Who Controls Your Child?

Who Controls Your Child?

Orley R. Herron

Thomas Nelson Publishers
Nashville

To parents and children struggling for love. To my parents and my wife's parents, who showed us what good parenting really is. To my children, whose own actions were behind my every word. To the faculty of National College of Education, and to the memory of its founder, Elizabeth Harrison, whose concern for helping mothers and children still inspires us to try harder.

Scripture quotations are from the *King James Version* of the Bible.

Library of Congress Cataloging in Publication Data

Herron, Orley R
  Who controls your child?

   1. Children—Management. 2. Children's rights.
I. Title.
HQ769.H5164   649'.1   80-21110
ISBN 0-8407-5221-0

CONTENTS

PREFACE

As National College of Education approaches its centennial in 1986, it is fitting that a book be written about children's rights. It has been my privilege to accomplish this task.

In the process of preparing the manuscript, I became even more deeply committed to children and to their right to grow up healthy and happy. Oddly, perhaps, I was not a child-centered person years ago. But when I took over the presidency at National College—an institution dedicated to preparing tomorrow's teachers—my child-consciousness was raised.

I see this book as a manual for parents. I hope these pages will be a guide to every present and future mother and father concerned about losing control of their children. This book is not a carte blanche endorsement of the movement known as "children's rights"; rather, it is a careful examination of the malaise of leadership pertaining to our children.

PREFACE

No one could write a manuscript of this sort and remain neutral on the issues discussed. I have had to take difficult stands, some of which may be troublesome to a number of readers. But I want you to know I have made these judgments as an educator, a husband, a father, and a Christian.

On some pages you might accuse me of being radical; on others, of being old-fashioned. Happily, I am both.

I call for children's rights without deifying them; I call for parents' rights without exaggerating them. For I know that the bottom line is neither your rights nor my rights, but God's will.

O.R.H.
Spring, 1980

PART I

CHAPTER ONE

DEADLY TUG OF WAR

You are a good parent. You're not perfect, but you feed your children well, send them to school each day, see that they get plenty of sleep, and keep them out of serious trouble. You probably adhere to the premise that if you do a good job bringing up your kids, they'll turn out all right.

Perhaps that was true twenty years ago. But today, a myriad of forces are fighting for control of your child. We aren't sure what—or how—our children are being taught in school. We see them passive in front of the television, hypnotized by violence and distorted pictures of life. Religious cults threaten to suck our children into their path, as their numbers spiral phenomenally. Sexual permissiveness begins in elementary school, and we see children who still need mothering becoming mothers themselves.

We are witnessing an alarming change in value systems. In your home children may be regarded as precious and unique creations, but outside your door lie countless youngsters who are neglected, abused, and wasted.

Somewhere, right now, a child is dying. He may

live down the block. His bloated belly may be empty or his tiny frame may be ravaged by disease. His face may be bruised, his feet may be bare, and a tear may be running down his soft cheek. As child advocate Eda LeShan has said, "This is a terrible time to be a child."[1]

Children are caught in a deadly tug of war, pulled toward disaster from every side. They are virtually powerless against overwhelming forces, and it is to our shame that these forces originate in adult society.

A global view: cloudy

Throughout the world, children are being denied the right to grow up.

- In underdeveloped countries, less than one third of the school-age population is in school.
- In some developing countries, 25 to 30 percent of the children die before they are five.
- Nutritional deficiency is responsible for as many as 57 percent of all deaths before age five.
- In developing countries there is only one doctor for every 3,700 people.
- Decent housing, caring families, and equal opportunity are illusions for millions.[2]

In our own country, the state of our children is startling.

- One of every two black preschool children lives in poverty.
- Poor children's chances of dying in their first year of life are two thirds greater than those of children living above the poverty level.

14

- One white student drops out for every four who graduate from high school, but one black child drops out of school for every two who graduate.
- 18.3 million American children under seventeen have never seen a dentist.
- 9.5 million children under eighteen have no regular source of primary health care.
- Only one in seventeen American families represents the typical image, with a working father, a stay-at-home mother, and two children.[3]

As the most privileged nation in the world, we still lag scandalously behind less privileged countries with respect to our youth. Says Pat Wald, staff attorney for the Mental Health Law Project (Washington, D.C.): "Despite the fact that more than 40 percent of Americans living at the poverty level are children and only 15 percent are over 65, we spend many more of our tax dollars on the aged than on youth."[4]

Every year Americans spend more money on dog food than on baby food. U.S. Senator Ernest Hollings of South Carolina declared in *The Case Against Hunger:*

It is now documented that from 10 to 15 million Americans are hungry constantly and chronically. They are Americans—not Biafrans, or those poor starving Chinese we all heard about in our childhood when we were being encouraged to clean our plates. They are in all corners of America and in every color—2 to 1, white over red and black.[5]

How many of those starving people are children? Are they being denied a share in the wealth and sustenance of this land simply because they are too young for their voices to be heard?

Tommy and Mary Ann

It's too easy to ignore a problem when we talk about faceless children. Give them names and the problem is real. Call one "Tommy."

Tommy was one of those babies everyone called " a perfect child." He had a pleasant disposition, and at six months he seldom cried. So neighbors were surprised when they heard him crying for a very long time. After three days, their surprise turned to concern. When no one answered the door at Tommy's home, neighbors called the police.

The officer who forced open the door was an eleven-year veteran of the police force, but when he saw Tommy in his crib, he vomited. The child was curled up in the corner of his crib, surrounded by bowls of soured milk and hardened baby food. He was in front of an open window, but the stench was terrible. He was covered with urine and feces, and he was turning blue.

When Tommy's mother returned four days later, she was furious that anyone would dare remove her baby from her apartment, and she threatened to sue. Tommy spent three weeks in the hospital, where he was treated for exposure, dehydration, and pneumonia. Doctors suspected brain damage.[6]

Call one "Mary Ann." Mary Ann was thirteen. One day she threw a snowball at an elderly neighbor. Mary Ann was arrested and charged with assault and battery. A check of her school records added truancy to her "crimes." Mary Ann was taken to a Youth Study Center—a prison by any other name.

All girls held in detention in the Youth Study Center were subjected to an internal vaginal examination to check for hidden drugs or weapons. Mary Ann flatly refused to allow the search. The Center refused to release her until she permitted the search. Her mother appealed to the law but found no sympathy. Petitions were presented and denied. Some courts would not docket the petitions. Apparently, the state did not regard Mary Ann as important.[7]

In Tommy's case we have a clear example of parental neglect. In Mary Ann's case we have an invasion of a young girl's constitutional right to privacy in the most extreme sense. Who was at fault in these cases? Who has authority over our children? And what rights do our children have?

Can rights undo the wrongs?

Only recently have some of us acknowledged the concept of children's rights. In the past, children "belonged" to parents and played no role in determining their own destiny.

A child has no say whether he will be born, or to whom. He cannot determine whether he will be a "wanted" child. If his parents so choose, they can put him up for adoption at birth. If he is handicapped, his parents can order him institutionalized. If he is severely disabled at birth, the doctors and his parents may decide to allow the child to die. If he is abused or neglected he may complain of it to someone, but he has no legal recourse. If he is ill, he may not obtain medical or psychiatric help without his parent's approval.

A child may have to hand over his wages if he has a job. He has no credit rating. He may not have the power to help choose his clothes or his education. He may be required to undergo serious surgery or treatment with mind-altering drugs without being asked or even told of the treatment. He cannot control access to his room or his school locker. He cannot ensure privacy of school or medical records, even though they may contain information that could restrict his options later in life.

The range of issues and the examples are infinite. Even in the field of medicine—the Hippocratic oath notwithstanding—abuses abound. In one instance, doctors wished to test their suspicion that a drug used to treat infections might also produce liver damage. They administered the drug to fifty healthy youngsters at a children's center, and a high incidence of hepatic dysfunction resulted. Eight children with marked dysfunction were transferred to a hospital, where biopsies verified the liver damage. After the liver function tests of this group had returned to normal, the drug was administered again to four of the children to confirm the results of the tests.[8]

What kind of society allows this to happen?

"Children don't count"

At the same time, we refuse to help millions of children who struggle against poverty, inflation, and unemployment. We shun involvement and responsibility in issues of education, juvenile justice, and child neglect. The Children's Defense Fund's three-year study, "Children Without Homes," showed that over one-half million children were living away from their families in situations ranging from foster homes to institutions. The study concluded:

> *Families don't count.* Funds and services neither encourage nor ensure parent-child contact.
> *Children don't count.* Thousands are haphazardly and inappropriately placed.
> *Children are lost.* They may have no assigned caseworker.
> *Children are faceless.* Child welfare officials know little about the children for whom they are responsible.
> *Children are forgotten.* Monitoring and review procedures are inadequate.
> *Children's needs are ignored by state and federal governments.*[9]

Children continue to be regarded as quasi-citizens, not quite able to share in those rights guaranteed by the Constitution. This statement from the New York State legislature is right on target:

> There is no one, and no one agency in government, to speak solely for the needs of children. From the highest to the lowest levels of government no one speaks on behalf of the overall needs of the child. The thousands of children who rely upon the child welfare

complex for care, treatment and protection are un-represented in government planning circles.[10]

Who will take a stand?

There was a time when parents and the family represented the children and cared for their needs. It may come as a surprise to those of us who are responsible parents, but we can no longer rely on the family to care for the nameless, faceless little ones. Do children, then, need their own bill of rights? In *Escape from Childhood,* John Holt proposes that we give young people the right to:

- equal treatment at the hands of the law
- be legally responsible for one's life and actions
- work for money
- privacy
- financial independence and responsibility
- direct and manage one's education
- travel, live away from home, choose or make one's own home
- receive from the state whatever minimum income it may guarantee to adult citizens
- seek and choose guardians other than one's own parents.[11]

In other words, Holt would give children the right to do what any adult may legally do. Children's rights advocates believe that nothing short of complete self-determination by the child is acceptable.

Then there are other concerned adults who declare loudly that parents, schools, churches, and courts are clearly responsible for children.

I will say now, and many times throughout the pages ahead, that *parents* are the answer. Parents should have the sensitivity to balance their children on that delicate and precarious perch between too many and too few rights. In this book I will give you, as a parent, a look at the key issues involving children's rights. I will begin with some hard questions that may be unpleasant; nevertheless, I urge you to confront them.

- When your child came into the world, you knew it was up to you to guide him, to help him develop into a mature, responsible adult and unleash his greatest potential. How much do you know about being a parent, about the stages of development your child goes through, and about what you need to do to help him through the trying times? Are you providing him an environment that encourages creativity, or one that unintentionally stifles it? Are you letting television be his teacher, companion, and parent? Do you practice informed obedience, or do you expect respect by decree?
- Are you thrusting your own frustrations on your children without meaning to? Do you fear you will resort to physical violence? Does your child need help or do you?
- How much does your child know about his own sexuality? Is your own embarrassment inhibiting his healthy development? Do you oppose sex education because you think sex will "go away" if you ignore it?
- Your child will receive the best education possible only if you and his teachers work together as

partners. Given the myriad problems of today's public schools, it is vital that education occur inside the home as well as in the classroom. Are you taking an active part in your child's learning process? Do you have a "special child" who needs special attention? Are you trying to understand your child's individual learning style?

- Are you giving your child moral education as well? Do you insist that your child go to church? Are spiritual lessons taught in your home? Do you think your child is invulnerable to the devilish powers of religious cults?

- Do you consider your children an intrusion or a blessing? Many couples today marry for all the wrong reasons—money, status, spite, impulsiveness, sex—and their reasons for having children are just as unsound. Husbands and wives, remember that from the moment of conception you are bringing a unique *person*, a child created by God, into this world. He deserves to be cherished.

But children are *not* adults. They do not spring forth fully grown and fully responsible. They must be cared for and cared about by parents who face the most important job of their lives. As your children grow, weigh the issues carefully. Whose hand will be rocking the cradle?

CHAPTER TWO

THE THREE Bs OF CHILD ABUSE: BEATEN, BRUISED, AND BURNED

When the policeman entered the house, he found Jenny tied to a bedpost. She had been beaten beyond description and was near death. Scrawled on a piece of paper beside her was the plea, "Mommy, if I die, will you love me?" She died three hours later.

In another community, Danny died too. The officer who found him lying on the floor was absolutely stunned that so much brutality could be inflicted upon such a small boy. The note near the child read, "Mom, I'm sorry for not cleaning up. I love you."

Jimmy's case is only slightly less tragic, even though he had dozens of toys, was well fed, and lived in a $250,000 house. Rather, I should say, his parents lived in a $250,000 house. Jimmy ate, slept, and played in a closet for two years.

The stories can go on as unmercifully as the beatings that occur each year in *one out of five American homes.* One of your neighbors might be killing his son or daughter as you read this chapter. Most likely, you have never abused your child. But how close have you come? Have you not been frightened at times by the power of your fury, by the potential for injury that lies in a fit of rage?

Child abuse is rising to epidemic proportions; soon it may be the leading cause of childhood death, topping the combined death totals from smallpox, polio, typhoid fever, and scarlet fever.

An estimated one million children are abused in the United States each year. Two to four thousand die—and those are only the ones we can count![1]

Children are beaten, scalded, boiled, blinded, raped, whipped, bludgeoned, hurled down stairs, and slashed with razor blades in a country that claims to place children and the family on a pedestal. What more abhorrent violation of a child's rights can we find than the instance where a three-year-old boy's fingernails were ripped off by his angry father? What is more loathsome than the case of a child whose father burned the words "bad boy" into his back with lighted cigarettes?

We can all agree that child abuse of any kind— physical, sexual, emotional, or through neglect—is intolerable and inexcusable. We can shake our heads over the more than 50,000 children who died from abuse in the 1970s alone, and the 300,000 who were permanently injured.[2] But I hear little national outcry in protest. I see no tide of letters flooding Washington. I see only the further disintegration of the American family, which I believe is largely responsible for this youthful holocaust. We are losing control.

We are now a nation of "lock-and-key" babies and "latch-key children." They are the babies whose mothers leave them unattended; they are the children who go off to school with house keys dangling from their necks. In our nation, 27 million children under the age of eighteen have mothers who work; 6 million are under five; and we have day-care facilities for less than 1 million.[3]

In our nation the roles of mother and father are not held in high esteem; the roles of the rich, the powerful, and the "successful" are. We live with violence, in the media and on the streets. We spend millions on juvenile detention, far less on detection of social problems. It costs $12,000 to keep a teenager in jail for one year; it costs far less to be a parent.[4]

The abusers

I believe that nearly all parents innately love their children. A high percentage of abusive parents were abused or neglected as children and know no other kind of parenting. They cannot cope with a web of financial, psychological, and social problems, and they don't know how to cry for help. They are white, black, Catholic, Protestant, under thirty, over fifty, highly educated, disadvantaged, or wealthy. They are garbagemen, engineers, doctors, electricians, carpenters, lawyers, and ministers. The myth that child abuse happens mainly among the lower classes is being shattered. It happens among all classes, but the middle and upper classes are more adept at keeping their atrocities secret.

I read of one case in which a prominent minister sexually abused his nine-year-old daughter. The act set off a family chain reaction of repeated sexual abuse before one family member finally sought help via an anonymous hotline.[5]

What, then, sets the stage for child abuse?

According to the National Committee for the Prevention of Child Abuse, child abuse is most likely to occur when . . .

. . . an adult has the potential to abuse. This often stems from the fact that he was abused by his parents, he is isolated from friends, he dislikes himself, he is unable to meet his own emotional needs, and he has no emotional support.

. . . he views the child as "special" or different. The child may seem too active or too passive; the child may be the result of an unwanted pregnancy or have a birth defect.

. . . there is a crisis or a series of crises. Even a car that won't start can be enough to trigger an abusive episode.[6]

In the case of incest, the key factors appear to be the parent's poor self-concept and poor sexual identification. In many cases, the abused child may have an unusually strong need for love and caring, and the only apparent source may be the molesting parent.[7] Psychologists estimate that as much as 10 percent of the population may have known an incestuous relationship.

The most commonly reported form of incest is between father and daughter. In many of these cases,

26

the father is a cruel disciplinarian, an obsessive-compulsive man from a broken home who seeks power over women.[8]

In one case, a man physically abused his daughter as an infant, then idealized and overprotected her until she was raped on the street at age eight. His rage and grief were compounded by his feeling, "They have taken my little virgin from me."[9]

A daughter may also become a replacement for her mother. One fourteen-year-old girl became her father's sexual partner when her mother was paralyzed from the waist down in an auto accident. The girl finally ran away from home at eighteen.[10]

In light of these examples and others too scandalous to mention, I am horrified when I read about the new "pro-incest" movement. Sexual researchers on the fringes of reason suggest that opposition to incest is like religious intolerance, and that sex between children and adult family members can be beneficial. Children's rights extremists say children should be allowed to express themselves sexually in any manner they choose.

I reject and condemn these arguments passionately, and I assume any reasonable parent would do the same. These simplistic, ludicrous justifications for incest ignore evidence of the resultant severe psychological and emotional harm to children. I must refute the pro-incest lobbyists with outrage and with pity.[11]

I feel pity, too, for the abusers, who need as much help as the abused. Hear the pain of this mother:

A lot of times, I hoped somebody would have caught up with me. I was sending her to school with black and blue marks all over her and she couldn't sit down. But the schools never said nothing [sic]. It really seemed like they could have cared less. It was only when I moved out to the suburbs that the schools caught up with me.

I thought I was the lowest-down s.o.b. that could ever walk, to harm my child that way. After I beat her, I felt guilty the whole damn day. . . .

A foster parent says:

I loved those kids very much when they were with us. It was like they were mine. The abuse was totally aside from whether or not I loved them.[12]

The children, of course, bear the physical and psychological scars. They grow older and turn to drug abuse, alcohol, prostitution, religious cults, and violent crime. According to *The Center* magazine:

A leading investigative psychologist has found a high degree of correlation between juvenile delinquency and the delinquents' having experienced brutal beatings from their parents in the first ten years of their lives. Out of the great pool of our neglected and battered children come significant numbers who will be involved in violent crime.[13]

Who saves the children?

We are doing little that effectively prevents abuse or helps its victims. Proper parental control is being lost by default. When we discover cases of child abuse or neglect, we rush to remove the child from the home and place him in foster care, an alternative that often is no better and one that can be emotionally destructive. If they do not enter foster care, the children may be returned to their parents without any kind of corrective action being taken. The parents resume their abuse, and the children move another step closer to total physical and emotional destruction.

Illinois spends millions of dollars on prisons, yet the budget for the Department of Children and Family Services has remained unchanged in recent years, despite an increase of reported abuses from 1,200 to 6,000. Bills dealing with the problem of teen-age runaways, venereal disease, increased day-care facilities, and juvenile delinquency remain bogged in bureaucracy. When money is spent, it goes toward treatment rather than prevention.[14]

The "superkids" excuse

There are a number of esteemed behavioral scientists who say that children can survive and succeed in spite of unfortunate circumstances, that childhood troubles have no long-range impact, and that there are "superkids" who will survive against all odds.

Harvard psychologist Jerome Kagan, one of the world's leading authorities on child development, says his new discoveries "imply that his [the human infant's] first experiences may be permanently lost.

. . . I suspect that it is not until a child is five or six years old . . . that we get a more reliable preview of the future. The infant's mind may be more like a sandy beach on a windy day than a reel of recording tape."[15]

In *Psychology Today*, research psychologist Arlene Skolnick of Berkeley's Institute of Human Development writes that it is a myth that children are vulnerable, particularly to the blunderings of parental guidance. She says that most child care advice "places exaggerated faith not only in the perfectibility of children and their parents but in the infallibility of the particular childrearing techniques."[16]

I disagree vehemently with these conclusions. Far too much evidence supports a child's vulnerability. If we let irresponsible parents go on their merry way, only to find out later that these new theories are wrong, what do we do then? How do we recapture someone's unfortunate childhood? This sort of reasoning only serves to let selfish and careless parents, teachers, and community leaders off the hook.

Analyst Gilbert W. Kliman of the New York Psychoanalytic Society has said:

> We in our culture are finding it increasingly difficult to bear the pain of our children . . . . So we must rationalize our collective neglect of children by denying that the neglect does them any harm. Just as each of us has individually repressed all the painful memories of those earliest most vulnerable years, we would like to be able to say of children in general: Early experience doesn't matter. It all just goes away and is forgotten.[17]

THE THREE Bs OF CHILD ABUSE

Some corrective steps

What should or can be done about child abuse? Whose responsibility is it? Parents'? Society's? The churchs'? The schools'?

Should punishment be used to deter child abuse?

Should society intervene when the likelihood of abuse appears great?

1. I believe that as a first step, couples should be counseled before they marry. Ministers should not hesitate to ask prospective husbands and wives about their childhoods and to probe for abuse in their pasts. No couple should enter into marriage without knowing if one or the other was an abused child, for it will have a significant effect on their marriage and on any children they may have.

2. When abuse is discovered in the home, parents should be counseled and then fined, as is done in England, before we resort to incarceration. Society must intervene to save the children.

I am well aware that the state's right to poke its nose into citizens' lives has always been questioned. But remember: We do not question civil laws protecting us adults. As *Children Today* magazine put it, "If an adult holding a large stick threatens to beat another adult, he may be guilty of assault. Yet this is a fairly common experience for many children. Should we give to children the same protection we give to adults, who are presumably more able to defend themselves?"[18]

3. The church must step in and tell its people how to raise their children when the children's lives

31

are in danger. I believe the church has become too passive in dealing with its troubled members— many of whom are crying out for help. And this opinion is certainly not mine alone. Well-known, Christian child expert Dr. James Dobson writes, "It is clearly the task of the Church to assist you with your parenting responsibilities."[19]

4. As an educator, I lay a major responsibility on the schools. During the past few years there has been a significant increase in schools' attempts to identify victims of child abuse and neglect. Many school districts are adopting policies that require teachers and other school district personnel to report suspected abuse and neglect. I applaud this protection and urge parents to push for similar programs in their community schools.

School administrators are instituting in-service educational programs for teachers and are joining with community action programs. Some are even teaching children about preventing child maltreatment. State legislatures are making some effort by providing mandates in state school codes for teachers to report suspected cases of abuse and protecting teachers against parental intimidation.

I believe there are thousands of caring teachers across America who are concerned about child abuse. Teachers must be involved whenever the learning process is impaired; battered, neglected children cannot grow intellectually.

5. We need *parent training courses* in every high school, college, and church. Courses on the de-

velopment of infants, preschoolers, and adolescents should be built into the curriculum of every Sunday school. Public television should offer courses on successful parenting. Family doctors should provide literature on rearing children.

We need greater family support systems. In many black, urban communities, grandmothers care for the babies of teen-aged mothers, and children know they can rely on a neighbor if a parent becomes too abusive. Not only do we need extended families, but we need to strengthen the nuclear family.

6. I do not oppose the right of women to work, but I do believe a mother should be with her child as much as possible during the first four years of his life. Less than that is a compromise no family can afford!

Historian Will Durant calls this the age of "the industrialization of woman.... Women call it emancipation because they wanted to do whatever the men did.... But it is a mistake to call that emancipation.... It will bring a good deal of suffering to women. But it's all in the nature of industrialization, which completes its work, and then has a nice big war, and begins all over again."[20]

We must count our families more important than career, power, and wealth. Intensely career-minded parents may be as guilty of child neglect as the parents who locked Jimmy in a closet. I know one man who refused four major job promotions because he did not want to move his family from a place where they were very happy. Hats off to him!

Hats off to all you good parents who have never and will never mistreat your children. I salute all of you who live with one thought uppermost in your mind: What is in the best interests of my child?

CHAPTER THREE

FOR THEIR OWN GOOD OR OURS?

Each year innumerable abuses occur that clearly violate the best interests of children. These are not the cases of beaten, bruised, and burned youngsters. No, these are cases of selfishness. Please pay careful attention to the warnings of this chapter, because we are dealing here with things that can happen to normal, middle-class families.

Our selfishness can range all the way from giving up an unwanted child to refusing a child medical treatment. Children take their problems to empty rooms and to housekeepers, while Mom and Dad are at the country club. My heart goes out to them as much as it does to the estimated 500,000 children in foster care, and to the millions whose lives are shattered by divorce. Who is taking a stand for our children's best interests, while the rest are "looking out for number one"?

Too much love

Five-and-a-half-year-old Laura might have been able to answer those questions. When Laura was thirteen months old, her unwed, eighteen-year-old mother placed her with the New York City Department of Welfare. Laura was subsequently transferred to the Jewish Child Care Association and placed in a foster home. The foster parents accepted Laura as a member of their family but agreed to permit some continuing relationship with Laura's natural mother.

During Laura's first year of foster care, her mother came to see her once. In three years, she came twice. The foster parents grew to love Laura and asked the agency to consider the possibility of legal adoption. The agency refused, and a court battle began between the agency and Laura's foster parents.

The agency's reasoning was nothing short of absurd. While acknowledging that the foster parents had provided Laura with a comfortable, loving home, the agency claimed Laura should be removed from their custody and placed in a "neutral environment." Laura's foster parents, you see, loved her too much. The court transferred Laura to a "neutral environment," despite a psychiatrist's testimony that stability was critically important to a child her age.[1]

The principle of "anti-attachment" won the case for the agency in the several appeals that followed. Laura lost. The dissenting judge anticipated the inevitable: multiple placements for Laura. He wrote:

If Laura is to be bandied about meanwhile from family to family until she is transferred to her mother, each such change will be extremely difficult for the child, as testified to without contradiction by the psychiatrist at the hearing. Why multiply the shocks? And if the mother never chooses to take Laura, and that does not appear to be unlikely from the record before us, the child could not find a better home than she now enjoys.[2]

Michael S. Wald of Stanford University wrote about attachment in a guest editorial in *Child Development.*

In one county I know, the person who runs the children's institution believes that because all of the children who come into the institution will eventually be returned to their parents or placed in foster care, the children should not develop any attachment relationships. She believes that it is bad to develop strong attachments which will later be disturbed. Accordingly she turned down an offer by a group of senior citizens to serve the children as foster grandparents, by visiting a specific child each day, because this would establish an attachment relationship.[3]

She believed her policy was in the best interests of the children.

Who spoke for Laura's best interests? What would she have chosen, if she could—"too much love" from her foster parents or a future of hopscotch affection? I would suggest one simple rule in Laura's case: People who love children should rear them, and children should have the right to remain with those they love.

WHO CONTROLS YOUR CHILD?

Legal kidnapping

Many years ago a very attractive young couple I knew took in a two-month-old boy whose mother gave him up. The couple were not able to have children and were overjoyed at becoming parents. When the child was five years old, his natural mother demanded that he be returned to her. The couple were beside themselves. It was as if a stranger had entered their home and tried to kidnap their son. Because they had never signed formal adoption papers, the court ruled that the boy must be returned to his blood mother.

For these loving friends, the memory of their son walking out the door is almost too much to bear, even now. "We'll never forget it," they told me. "He turned to us in desperation, wanting so badly to stay. We had to turn our backs on him." Let me ask again: What was in the best interests of that child?

Seventeen years later, the boy is still having emotional problems that stem from when he was yanked from the only home he knew. The boy has visited his foster parents in recent years, and still he asks, "Why did you let me go?" His feelings of rejection are deep and permanent. Should that boy have had the right to choose his home?

Every child in a similar situation would not be capable of making that kind of decision. Each case must be judged individually. But the judgment must be based on the best interests of the child, not on the letter of a law that violates a human right. Parents who choose to give up their children should not have the right to later force them from a loving home. Sometimes we must put the irresponsible parents' rights aside for the sake of the children.

Studies show that a minority of natural parents reclaim their children; more than 50 percent of children placed in foster care never return to their natural parents. Fewer than 5 percent of children in long-term foster care are eventually adopted. The greatest hindrance to such adoption is the difficulty of terminating the rights of the natural parents, despite evidence from scores of child psychologists and psychiatrists that multiple homes harm children. Legislators remain reluctant to liberalize termination laws, even though that would ease the way for adoptive parents.

Unlikely to be reclaimed by a natural parent, unable to be adopted because of legal ties to that parent, unable to form lasting relationships with foster parents because of anti-attachment principles, children like Laura begin to move from home to home, usually three or more. Each move contributes to the rootlessness and rejection that blackens their lives forever.

Let me emphasize that I would never side with libertarians who seek to pull children from normal homes with loving parents. Not for a minute am I ignoring the authority of the many concerned mothers and fathers.

But we must decide whether and when the rights of natural parents conflict with the best interests of the child. Goldstein, Freud, and Solnit, in *Beyond the Best Interests of the Child*, pose the possibility that in some cases either the natural or foster parent emerges as the "psychological parent" of the child, and that it may be in the child's best interests to place custody with that parent.[4] I would add that it is in the child's best interests to give him a part in that decision. I believe the same reasoning should hold true in the painful dilemma involving children of divorce.

Is shuttle custody the answer?

There are currently 12 million children under the age of eighteen whose parents are divorced. About a million children each year suffer through the breakup of their families. The number of children involved in divorce has tripled in the last twenty years. Albert Solnit, director of the Yale Child Study Center in New Haven, Connecticut, says, "Divorce is one of the most serious and complex mental health crises facing children of the 80s." Child psychologist Lee Salk calls divorce a trauma for children "second only to death."[5]

While child custody has historically, and usually automatically, gone to the mother, today fathers are demanding their rights, too. Frankly, I am happy to see that. The mother is not always the best parent.

Increasingly, though, parents are opting for joint custody. Such an arrangement, in which parents retain equal custody of the child and share equally in the provision of a home and time together, was virtually unheard of five years ago. Today, eight states have joint custody provisions. That distresses me, because with joint custody nobody is really in charge.

In one case, the son stayed Monday through Thursday with his mother and Thursday night through Sunday with his father. The advantage here was that the child did not envision himself as having "lost" a parent in the divorce.

In most cases, however, shuttle custody is objectionable. "You never feel permanent anymore," said a fifteen-year-old girl. "I feel like an animal with a mind. You have to spend so much time with each person. You go from place to place."

In the majority of custody cases today, the best interests of the children are still taking a back seat to the best interests of convenience, easy visitation privileges, or a parent's social life. We must start listening to the children. They will tell us, and they have a right to be heard.

Danger in toyland

In another children's rights issue, consider the case of three-year-old Kristen from Massachusetts. She was a much-wanted child; she had a right to life. And life to Kristen meant two important things: a very good friend and a new swing set. Every day Kristen and her friend would spend hours on the swing set.

One afternoon Kristen's mother heard a loud banging on the back door. When she answered it, she found Kristen's friend standing outside, looking very scared. Then she saw Kristen.

41

At the top of the slide attached to the swing set there was a handrail that ended with a vertical post instead of a curved, closed handrail. The post had become entangled in Kristen's clothing and she had lost her balance, fallen off the slide, and hanged herself.[6]

How many other Kristens were there? Who thought about the best interests of the child when the swing set was designed? Was the manufacturer attempting to shave costs, or was the straight post a deadly oversight? The manufacturer later took that swing set model off the market.

There are three rights involved in this case: The manufacturer's right to advertise and sell his product; Kristen's parents' right to expect that the product would be safe; and Kristen's right to live. I don't believe any company would intentionally cause a child's death. But as parents we must work for stricter regulations governing the safety of toys and equipment for children. We must be painstakingly careful when we purchase products for our children. If the manufacturer passes the buck to the parent, and we parents pass it on to "society," it will stop with the children.

Pedaling to disaster

Rickie, fourteen, died in Escalon, California, when he was a high school freshman. Police officers reported that Rickie had been riding his bicycle at a high rate of speed on Highway 120. Rickie's bike, which had racing tires, skidded on a rain-slick road, and Rickie lost control. He was tossed forward into a parked car, and from there he bounced into the path of a passing truck.

Highway 120 was an extremely busy highway. For years town officials had tried to reroute it around the city. According to the Escalon Chamber of Commerce, the city had been "continually pressuring our State Legislature for the completion of a bypass." However, funds had been diverted toward completion of the interstate system, despite the fact that the stretch of Highway 120 through Escalon had accounted for *186 other accidents and 4 other fatalities in a three-year period!* Rickie still might have fallen had there been a bypass, but the truck might not have crossed Rickie's path.[7]

Who is to blame? Rickie, for riding his bicycle recklessly? His parents, or his school, for failing to teach him about bike safety? The manufacturer, for selling slick racing tires? The state legislature, for failing to complete the bypass? Escalon city officials, for failing to exert sufficient pressure on their legislators?

The responsibility and the blame in this case is divided, but we parents are still the key. We cannot assume that others will do their part, and we cannot wait for the slow wheels of bureaucracy to turn. Two thirds of the bicycle deaths every year involve children ages five to fourteen, and 70 percent of all bicycle injuries are caused by falls. We are not teaching our children enough about bike safety. While we're blaming someone else, millions of children are breaking bones and facing paralysis, disfigurement, and death.

Labors without love

No one knows how many children are illegally employed in the United States, but it is estimated that the number may be as high as 600,000 at any one time. U. S. Department of Labor investigators find children as young as eleven working ten to fourteen hours a day and fifty to seventy hours a week, sometimes working until after midnight.

Despite child labor laws established years ago, children have been found working in freezer plants, slaughterhouses, sawmills, construction companies, chemical plants, log-driving companies, hamburger stands, motels, restaurants, and laundries— anywhere a company wants to save by paying low wages and avoiding Social Security taxes.

Even children who work legally are often unprepared for adult responsibilities. One sixteen-year-old boy, after three weeks on a summer job, was told by the adult in charge of the plant to drive a forklift truck. The boy had received no training in how to operate the hazardous equipment. He made a mistake in turning, tipped the truck over, and was crushed to death.

A fifteen-year-old boy working in the construction industry was buried in a twenty-one-foot sewer ditch when a section of the bank gave way. A thirteen-year-old working on an apartment building fell to his death from a balcony. A little girl working in the fields was literally scalped by a mechanical harvester.

I do not oppose the right of children to work and earn pay when they are old enough and ready for adult responsibilities. We must not, however, allow our own greed or that of others to govern our judgment. Say no if you think your child is too young to take a summer job. Pay him for jobs around the house. Teach children about values that are not tied to material wealth.

Of life and death

A final question that cannot be left untouched in a decision of children's best interests concerns medical treatment. What are the rights of a child in deciding whether or not to receive medical care? In the case of adults, the principle of "informed consent" holds true. A person gives permission in advance for medical treatment, and that permission must be given intelligently and with comprehension of the risks involved. Should a child have the same right?

Child advocate Pat Wald believes a child should begin to participate in medical decisions at the age of twelve.[8] The Carnegie Council on Children has recommended that the age when minors can seek medical treatment on their own be lowered from eighteen or twenty-one. "The exact age will have to be debated, but children of any age caught in desperate situations because of drugs or pregnancy should be able to consult a doctor without fear of exposure."[9]

Wald believes youth should have the right to refuse or resist treatment: "No more 'voluntary' commitments by parents of their children to mental hospitals; no more 'voluntary' sterilizations of retarded youth, parent-compelled abortions, psychosurgery or other risky surgical or experimental procedures."[10]

In cases where the ravages of disease or the severity of an injury cast doubt on a child's ability to make a rational decision, outside agencies may have to interfere. A weakened, frightened youngster may refuse surgery after an auto accident, but as a parent I could not grant him the right to make that decision.

I believe children should be able to participate in medical decisions to the greatest degree of which they are intellectually and emotionally capable, even before the age of twelve. And in cases where parents' personal or religious beliefs interfere with a child's medical treatment, I side with the child. As a Christian, I would plead with these parents to believe that God can use medical science to heal the sick, and not to deny children the care that could save their lives.

New laws and court decisions are moving in the direction of children's rights. In some states minors have the right to medical help without their parents' knowledge or consent. At least forty-eight states grant such freedom when a teen-ager has a venereal disease; some states extend it to pregnancy, abortion, contraception, drug addiction, mental disorders, or severely contagious diseases. In Maryland, the Court of Appeals has upheld the right of a sixteen-year-old girl to refuse to have an abortion ordered by her parents. In Mississippi, any child can make medical decisions as long as he or she is "of sufficient intelligence to understand and appreciate the consequences."

I recognize the complexity of the issues confronted in this chapter, and I advise you to be ruled by your heart if you are faced with a painful choice involving a child. Let one thought be your guide: Are you acting for the child's own good, or for your own?

CHAPTER FOUR

DOUBLE STANDARDS OF JUSTICE

If a son shall ask bread of any of you that is a father, will he give him a stone? Or if he ask a fish, will he for a fish give him a serpent?

—Luke 11:11

Mark that passage well, for it tells us something about our society today. Take a close look and you'll see a court system where fairness is still dragging behind. You'll see courts that have ceased to serve the people and instead are inquisitors to whom the rest of society must answer. Those two questions that Jesus asked are centuries old, but in our society we are still giving our children stones and serpents—with legal sanction.

It has only been in the last fifteen years that the law has recognized children as people, entitled to constitutional rights and freedoms that adults take for granted. The legal victories have been piecemeal and painfully late. Children's rights have been consistently denied, by design as well as by ignorance. Children have been the basketballs of bureaucracy

48

and the pawns of a society that is unwilling or unable to deal with their troubles. How far have we come since ancient Roman parents legally committed infanticide? How far have we come since English fathers sold their children into slavery?

Cruel, but not unusual, punishment

We need not search the dusty history books to find examples of juvenile injustice. We need only go back to 1964, when the sheriff of Gila County, Arizona, arrested fifteen-year-old Gerald Gault.[1] Gerald, who was on six months' probation for being in the company of a friend who stole a wallet, was accused of making an obscene phone call to his neighbor. Gerald knew he had only dialed the number—his friend had done the talking—but that plea would go unheard throughout the nightmare that followed.

Gerald asked the sheriff if he could call his parents or leave a note to tell them his arrest. His request was denied, and he was taken to the children's detention home.

When Gerald's parents arrived home that evening, they looked frantically for their son until they learned from friends where he had been taken. They received no explanation for the charge against Gerald, and no notice of the accusation, which said merely: ". . . said minor is under the age of 18 years, and is in need of the protection of this Honorable Court and said minor is a delinquent."

At a hearing in juvenile court the next day, the complainant was not present and neither were her charges in writing. The brief session was conducted shabbily, with no records kept, and Gerald spent two more days in the detention home before he was released. A second hearing one week later was as scandalously unjust. Again, the complainant did not appear, nor was there a record of the judge having contacted her. The sole evidence against Gerald was his probation officer's report. The charge: lewd phone calls.

Had this case involved an adult defendant, the fine would have ranged from five to fifty dollars, with a maximum of two months in jail. But the judge sentenced Gerald to six years in reform school.

The Supreme Court ruled in Gerald's favor in 1967, and he was released. But three years had passed, and he was already scarred.

It took the highest court in the land to rule that Gerald, and other children like him, were human beings. The court stated, ". . . neither the Fourteenth Amendment nor the Bill of Rights is for adults alone. We are to treat the child as an individual human being and not revert in spite of good intentions to the more primitive days when he was treated as chattel." The landmark decision established the right of children to due process—the right to have notice of the charges, the right to counsel, and the right to be protected against self-incrimination.

In a country built on the cause of freedom and human dignity, Gerald Gault was accorded fewer rights for his wrongful adolescent prank than a hardened criminal would have been given automatically. Ask yourself: Who was in control in this matter?

Gerald's case is not uncommon. It reflects a juvenile court system beset by major difficulties. According to the National Crime Commission Report issued the year of Gerald's arrest, only 213 of 2,987 juvenile court judges were full-time professionals. Half of those judges did not hold undergraduate degrees. One fifth had no college education. One fifth were not members of the bar. One fourth had no legal training. In addition, most of the judges and courts had no psychological or psychiatric help available, and one third had no probation or social officers. During the following year, approximately 700,000 delinquency cases were disposed of in juvenile courts. "Disposed" is unfortunately an all too accurate word here, for the juvenile justice system has thrown away countless young lives in the years since its inception.

"Benevolent parent" fails

When the juvenile court system was established in 1899 in Chicago's Cook County, it was a welcome and heartening breakthrough as a new way to treat delinquent children.[2] For years, children charged with minor offenses had been imprisoned with dangerous adult criminals, where they became the playthings of sexually aggressive offenders. Children "matured" out of fear, learning coping skills based on criminal values. They were returned to

51

society as hardened, damaged children, and their minor offenses were later magnified many times over.

The juvenile court system was created to bring care and concern to children who needed legal reinforcement to adjust to a changing society. The court was to act as a "benevolent parent" who could guide wayward youth toward productive futures. Love, attention, fairness, and cooperation were to be the hallmarks of this new system. It would bring hope and resolve to minors caught in the quicksand of decaying cities, changing suburbs, and broken homes.

The juvenile court was to be a setting for mediation, and as such it bore little resemblance to adult criminal courts. Customary rules of evidence, probable cause, guilt beyond a reasonable doubt, and the right to counsel were eliminated. Hearings were closed to the public, and the court's decisions could not be appealed.

Those finely laid plans went awry. "The juvenile court judge became an all-powerful figure, who decided the fates of those brought before him on the basis of his training (which was sometimes minimal or unrelated to work with juveniles), previous experience, and impressions of the amenability of each child to various forms of treatment."[3]

In a system that quickly became overburdened, children were placed on a judicial assembly line that left little room for counseling and individual attention. Youngsters branded as "delinquents" sank deeper into despair. According to juvenile counselors, "Children who have been judged as delinquent, and their families, have begun to forfeit the right to make their own decisions. The youngsters are approaching a downward escalator that can lead them to complete control inside an adult prison, and perhaps to personal oblivion."[4]

Status offenders

The saddest cases are those of the "status offenders," children whose "crimes" would not be considered illegal for adults. They are disobedient, they run away from home, they skip school, they loiter in taverns and pool halls. Kenneth Keniston writes in *All Our Children*, "Jails, detention homes, and training schools are filled with 'rebellious' children whose only crime has been disobedience. . . ." He says there are 100,000 youths placed in adult jails or police lockups every year.

A New York State survey showed that 43 percent of the children in jail were status offenders.[5] One nationwide survey of institutionalized juveniles revealed that 75 percent of females and 25 percent of the males had committed status offenses.[6] These are the kids whose parents have set aside their responsibilities as mothers and fathers and sentenced their children to an uncertain, if not miserable, young adulthood.

More often than not, it is the parents who have driven the children to rebellion. "Disinterested, physically abusive, disturbed, alcoholic, or neglectful parents can create home situations that make school achievement or meaningful day-to-day existence virtually impossible for the children under their care," says a recent article in *Intellect* magazine. "Runaway behavior, particularly by girls, is frequently a cry for help or even the most reasonable solution to a dangerous or unbearable home situation."[7]

How quickly we are willing to abandon our children and blame them for our own mistakes! As I have said before, a child does not "sour" overnight; he collects years of neglect and mistreatment before his pain surfaces as extreme disobedience. Parents and the courts are all too eager to assume the worst without looking for the best. The benefit of the doubt and second chances are dispensed with rarity.

In one case, a high school senior who had completed all but two months of her probation for shoplifting was suddenly accused of stealing $8 at school. The principal threatened to have her arrested and her probation extended, coerced her into signing a confession and replacing the money, and forbade her to attend the senior prom. No witnesses were produced, nor formal hearing conducted. No parents came forward to uphold their daughter's rights.[8]

In one community, the Boys Club refuses membership to delinquent boys. Some medical doctors refuse to examine unmarried youthful offenders for pregnancy. It seems that juvenile justice is only for adults. Juvenile laws have been written for adults who want perfect children, mini "grown-ups." We deny children's *human* rights as we strip them of their legal rights.

DOUBLE STANDARDS OF JUSTICE

Children are persons

A 1969 Supreme Court decision is considered the "American Revolution" of children's legal rights. And although that Independence Day of February 24, 1969, was more than a decade ago, its mandate still goes ignored too often.[9]

We can review the case with more objectivity in the 1980s, for we educators of the 1960s were caught up in the emotional turbulence of the war in Viet Nam. The case points out how reasonable people can become unreasonable and irrational. It shows how we must protect each other against overreacting. It affirms that individual expression cannot be denied, regardless of a person's age.

Tinker vs. Des Moines does not involve juvenile delinquents, but the children of respected families. Two of the three were the son and daughter of a Methodist minister. All three were to become the interest of the nation and our highest court.

John Tinker, fifteen, his sister, Mary Beth, thirteen, and Chris Eckhart, sixteen, of Des Moines, Iowa, wanted to protest the Viet Nam war by wearing arm bands to school and fasting for two days. When school officials learned of the proposed protest, they quickly instituted a new regulation: Anyone wearing arm bands to school would be suspended. Furthermore, the student could not return unless he came without the arm band. Aware of the new rule, John, Mary, and Chris came to school wearing arm bands.

Let me say in all candor that in 1969, operating on

the information I had, I was most suspicious of the anti-war movement and was politically on the side of these school officials in Des Moines. Had the three been wearing a political campaign button, an Iron Cross (a German medal for wartime bravery), or any one of many other symbols, they would have made no waves. But their position on the Viet Nam war was generally unpopular. It made school officials uncomfortable. No doubt their discomfort was even greater when the case reached the Supreme Court.

The court ruled that students did not "shed their constitutional rights of freedom of speech or expression at the school-house gate" and that one symbol—the arm band—could not be singled out for prohibition. "In our system . . . schools may not be enclaves of totalitarianism," wrote the court. And, in the most dramatic statement, the court said, "Students in school as well as out of school are 'persons' under our Constitution." Just as children were *human beings* in the Gault case, they were *persons* in the Tinker case. Statements of the obvious? One would have thought so.

In a later case (Goss vs. Lopez, 1975), the court spelled out "minimum procedures" to be followed when students are suspended for up to ten days. Students must be given "some kind of notice," "some kind of hearing," oral and written notification of the charges, an explanation of the evidence, and a chance to present their side of the story.[10]

Educators should be especially sensitive to children's rights and needs. A study by the National Education Association's Bicentennial Committee revealed that youths most want their teachers to "understand how they feel and to help them learn how to cope in the world." Yet in another study, 81 percent of the high school students questioned felt teachers did not respect their opinions.[11] Teachers who violate their students intellectually commit a type of abuse as inexcusable as physical abuse.

"Seat-of-the-pants" discipline

Only poorly trained educators, I believe, resort to maintaining order by the seats of their students' pants. There are many, many documented cases of children who have been injured by severe beatings after being denied the opportunity to explain an infraction. A 285-pound former football player who taught at a state boys' school used to strike students up to fifteen times with a "fraternity stick."

Russell Baker, who lived in Gibbonville, North Carolina, was spanked on the buttocks by his teacher because he broke a rule against throwing kickballs.[12] His mother took the case to court. In 1973, the landmark case reached the Supreme Court, where the judges did not outlaw corporal punishment but outlined specific guidelines. The court said students should be warned in advance that spanking is the penalty for a certain violation, and that spanking should be a last-resort punishment, administered in the presence of another school staff member. Students could contest the punishment if they felt it unjust, the court said, and parents should receive a written explanation of their child's infraction.

Although I personally oppose corporal punishment in the classroom, I regard the Baker decision as a vote for children's rights. Four years later, however, the Supreme Court reached what I consider an alarming conclusion in another spanking case. The court decided that paddling could be administered even though it was medically harmful. I find that decision intolerable.

As I review the cases discussed in this chapter, I am not comforted. An emancipation proclamation for children has yet to be written.

A plea to parents

Children are entitled to the constitutional rights of adulthood and to the frailties of childhood. We must work to upgrade the training of those who administer justice, who rehabilitate delinquents, who educate children. We need new information systems, new standards of entry into these professions, and more in-service training.

But the most effective weapon against juvenile injustice is a caring home environment. If parents won't control their children, the court system will. The troubled child at home is the discipline problem in school and the one who reaches adulthood in detention. In one Chicago high school, I can trace nearly every disobedient, disrespectful, and delinquent child to one of eight families. It is in those kinds of families that juvenile reform must begin.

Parents, I urge you to keep your child out of the court system and at the same time to work for its improvement. Speak up through your parent organizations, through elected officials, and through government agencies. When cases of injustice occur, be persistent in your demands for fairness. When abuse of office is discovered on the court bench, in the social agency, or in the school system, a community outcry can spark major changes in the system.

Finally, call for the utilization of community resources that are consistently ignored. As enrollments decline, schools are closing and administrators are being laid off. We can use the schools twenty-four hours a day for our children's rehabilitation and growth. Schools can be centers for sports events, youth group meetings, tutoring, inexpensive movies, and a host of other activities every night of the week.

We can also use caring and competent teachers, administrators, and guidance counselors to replace the many poorly trained personnel in bureaucratic social agencies. Well-trained educators are eminently qualified to work with the poor, the elderly, the homeless, and the uneducated who suffer in the corners of every community.

CHAPTER FIVE

YOUR CHILD'S EDUCATION: ARE SCHOOLS AND PARENTS FLUNKING OUT?

School days, school days,
Good old-fashioned school days,
Readin' and 'ritin' and 'rithmetic,
All to the tune of a hickory stick . . .

Few people are singing that rhyme today, for we are in the age of "new-fashioned school days." The tune of the hickory stick may not be in harmony with parents any more, and education is too often bogged down in a quagmire of politics, bureaucracy, and budgets.

During twelve years of schooling a child spends more than 11,000 hours in the classroom. That classroom is no longer in a little red schoolhouse. The teachers are no longer bespectacled "old maid" school marms in high-collared dresses and orthopedic shoes.

In fact, today's Dick and Jane may go to a school where the teachers are out on strike. Or they may have to ride a bus for hours to get to school. A "secret file" on Dick and Jane may mention learning problems their parents know nothing about. Dick may be in a special program for the handicapped; Jane may be in one for the gifted.

We talk about "back to basics" today, but there's nothing basic about our modern educational system. It is hopelessly, horrendously, and pitifully complicated, and we cannot continue to let our children become tangled in that web. In the 1980s, it is critical that parents and schools work together as partners, not as adversaries who try to outdo one another in passing the educational buck back and forth.

Let us examine a number of explosive educational issues, where parents and/or schools may be flunking.

Striking out

At the beginning of the 1979-80 school year, nearly 8,000 teachers in eight states refused to show up for classes.[1] In early 1980, Chicago's 473,000 public school students got an unexpected vacation when 26,000 teachers virtually closed the school doors for more than a week.[2]

As school budgets tighten, more and more teachers will join the picket lines, and fewer and fewer students will receive the education they are entitled to. Children not only lose learning time while strikes are in progress, but they may also form negative attitudes about learning and toward teachers that could last far longer than the walk-outs. Strikes leave children confused and parents angry. Whether or not the teachers have legitimate grievances is moot; the question here is, where do the *children* take their grievances? What happens to their right to a quality education?

Teachers' strikes will be the educational crisis of this decade if we do not modify our present system. Although I know the tax base must be improved, I lay the major blame for this astonishing mess we're in at the feet of the local school boards.

Across the country we have school board members with minimal academic, administrative, and financial competence making major educational decisions and spending huge sums of money in the wrong places. Champions of brick and mortar slash valuable arts and extracurricular programs from the budget. Part-time volunteers ride out their terms on personal vendettas—to abolish a particular course or fire a superintendent. We are witnessing a tragedy, as one superintendent told me, where "personal will and private prejudice are becoming public policy in our schools."

I believe schools would fare far better without school boards. We need advisory committees instead—composed of professional educators, financially capable businessmen, and parents—to help govern our school systems. Many communities could tap the expertise of fine college and university faculties as well as bright business leaders.

But I am a realist, and I acknowledge that school boards are so firmly implanted in our bureaucracy that in all likelihood they will remain. The next best solution, then, is for parents to become more involved in school board elections so that those least qualified do not have a hand in children's education. If advisory committees cannot supplant school boards, they can perhaps supplement them in communities willing to make that commitment.

The buck starts here

Parents who are already involved in their children's learning processes are the ones who don't panic when strikes occur or when problems develop. They are the ones who already are taking an interest in their child's projects. They join the PTA and other parents' organizations; they schedule parent-teacher conferences when they have questions. They are unlike this parent of seven-year-old Joey:

> I can't be bothered going to parent-teacher conferences. I just don't have time. If Joey is having problems in school, I assume his teacher will let me know. The way I look at it, "No news is good news." So far, I haven't heard any complaints from Joey's teacher, so I don't see any reason for me to go to school.[3]

No reason? The parents of a California boy found their reason too late. They sued the school district because their son had graduated from high school with the ability to read at only the fifth-grade level.[4] The schools certainly share the blame in this case, but I first shake my finger at the parents. Where were they when the boy was learning to read? Where were they when he was in elementary school and junior high? Parents must supplement classroom instruction with the "three As" of learning—attention, affection, and approval.

WHO CONTROLS YOUR CHILD?

Learning in spurts

There are too many mysteries about the way children learn to place the sole responsibility of education on teachers. Recent research conducted by Dr. Conrad Toepfer, associate professor of middle-school education at the University of Georgia, is a perfect example.[5] Toepfer's theories are based on the work of Herman T. Epstein, professor of biology at Brandeis University, who discovered that the brain grows in stages.

As Table 1 shows, a child's brain experiences growth spurts at certain ages, and lags or plateaus at other times. From three to ten months, for example, the brain grows a great deal. From ten months to two years (indicated by a straight line on the graph), growth levels out and the brain takes a "rest." Other growth spurts are evident between two and four years, six and eight years, ten and twelve years, and fourteen and sixteen years. After the plateau period from ten months to two years, a parent can expect to see other lags between four and six years, eight and ten years, and twelve and fourteen years.

Toepfer says children, particularly in middle school, are often pushed into advanced academic tasks during plateaus, when they can't handle them. Children are inundated with calculus, physics, and chemistry when their brains need time to mull things over, to "consolidate, refine, and mature" skills already learned.

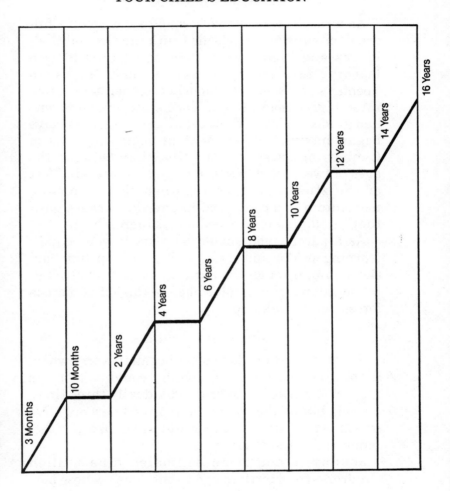

Table 1.
Childhood Brain Growth Pattern: Spurts and Plateaus

As a result, we see the "turn-off syndrome." Children's circuits are overloaded with intellectual challenges and high expectations until they blow a learning fuse and stop dead in their tracks. In Toepfer's study of four thousand students in a top-rated high school in New York state, students who had grades no lower than B-minus before age twelve began having achievement problems—grades of C-minus or lower—for the first time between the ages of twelve and fourteen (a plateau period). Most of the students never regained their learning momentum and continued to have low grades until they graduated or dropped out of high school.

As a parent, you should be alert to your child's learning peaks and valleys. Try to help him, not shove him, through the hard times. Get involved in his schooling. Get involved before the jolt of a crisis forces you to wake up.

The special child

Johnny's first-grade teacher began to worry when, despite her best efforts, Johnny couldn't learn to read. She worked with him individually three times a week, but by the end of the year he knew only five or six letter sounds and could recognize just his name and three other words.

Johnny is one of an estimated nine million children—from birth to age twenty-one—whose parents have a special reason to take part in their education. These children—more than 10 percent of the population in that age group—are physically, mentally, emotionally, or socially handicapped. Their educational needs are exceptional, and they require exceptional cooperation between parents and schools.

Parents of handicapped children get a double dose of problems. They experience all the responsibilities, joys, and sorrows that all parents deal with, along with shock, denial, depression, anger, guilt, grief, mourning, and finally, acceptance of the challenge before them. The quality of parenting—the day-to-day care, the education, and the training a special child receives—*can* make a difference.

Parents should be alert to early warning signals that might indicate problems in a very young child. The earlier a handicap is identified, the more successfully the problem can be handled. Table 2 lists some early warning signs that may point to a problem.[6]

In the past, parents have faced heartbreaking educational alternatives for handicapped children. One kindergarten child with a mild learning disability that caused him to be hyperactive was suspended from public school and received no education until first grade, when his parents enrolled him in a private school. Another family, whose daughter had cerebral palsy, was forced to move to a large city where the child could attend a private day school and receive other services through a university clinic. Other special children have been institutionalized as young adults because they received no special programming in school.

If your child does have a problem, you should know that he has as much right, by federal and state

Table 2.

Warning Signs of Possible Handicaps in Children*

SEEING	HEARING	TALKING
If your child . . .	If your child . . .	If your child . . .
—does not blink or turn head away from bright lights by two months . . .	—does not turn toward sounds by two months . . .	—is not babbling by six months . . .
—frequently rubs his eyes . . .	—stops making babbling sounds after having once started . . .	—does not respond to the spoken word by age one . . .
—has reddened, watering, or encrusted eyelids . . .	—has frequent ear aches or running ears . . .	—is not using single words by age two
—crosses one or both eyes . . .	—speaks always in a very loud or very soft voice . . .	—is not understood when talking by age three . . .
—holds head in an unnatural position when looking at something . . .	—tends to omit parts of words . . .	—is not talking in short sentences by age four . . .

MOVING

If your child . . .

—is unable to sit up
without support by age one . . .

—cannot walk without
help by age two . . .

—does not walk up and down
steps by age three . . .

—is unable to balance on
one foot for a short time
by age four . . .

—cannot throw a ball
overhand and catch a large
ball bounced to him/her
by age five . . .

PLAYING

If your child . . .

—does not play games
such as peek-a-boo, patty-
cake, or wave bye-bye by
age one . . .

—does not imitate parents
doing routine household
chores by age two to three . . .

—does not enjoy playing
alone with toys, pots and
pans, sand, etc., by
age three . . .

—does not play group
games such as hide-and-
seek, tag-ball, etc. with
other children by age four . . .

—does not share and
take turns by age five . . .

THINKING

If your child . . .

—does not react to his/her
own name when called by age one . . .

—is unable to identify hair,
eyes, ears, nose, and mouth by
pointing to them by age two . . .

—does not understand simple
stories told or read by age three . . .

—does not give reasonable
answers to such questions as,
"What do you do when you are
sleepy?" or "What do you do
when you are hungry?" by
age four . . .

—does not seem to understand
the meanings of the words
"today," "tomorrow," and
"yesterday" by age five . . .

69

*If you observe any of these signs in your child, consult a physician immediately.

laws, to a free and "appropriate" education as any other child. Public Law 94-142,* the Education for All Handicapped Children Act of 1975, guarantees your child's educational rights and your rights as parents to become involved in his learning process. It is a sad commentary on our educational system that we must have a law to insure this.

Frequently schools employ the concept of *mainstreaming*, or incorporating special children into the regular classroom for all or part of their school day. But mainstreaming has its problems. Many regular classrooms are not adequately equipped to meet the special child's needs. Further, some teachers, untrained in educating handicapped children, feel personally threatened by a role they cannot fulfill and feel that the presence of a special child in the classroom handicaps the learning of his classmates. And parents, who feel even more helpless, are faced with another of a long string of frustrations and doubts about this new "accommodation to learning."

The key lies in seeing that teachers are properly trained to work with mainstreamed students. It is estimated that nearly 80 percent of teachers currently employed would need additional training to meet the needs of special students.

Parents, be aware of this shift to mainstreaming,

---

*P.L. 94-142 covers an age range of three to twenty-one years in most states. Exceptions would occur in states where different age ranges are used for public education, as, for example, a state where the age range might be four to nineteen years.

and call for more in-service teacher education and for adequate funding for specially trained teachers and special programs for the handicapped. Be cautious about letting your embarrassment—the "stigma" of having a handicapped child—dictate whether mainstreaming is the best educational program for your child.

The gifted child

At the other end of the spectrum from the handicapped "special child" is the 3 to 5 percent of the school-age population who are considered "gifted"—about two million kids. These children can range from levels of two years ahead of their peers to near genius. But only 12 percent of gifted and talented children are receiving some kind of service or support. Perhaps that explains why some 20 percent of school dropouts in our country are thought to be gifted.

Schools have been slow to recognize that the gifted child has just as much right to a free and "appropriate" education as the handicapped child. In many cases parents have resorted to private schools or lawsuits to obtain a better education for their gifted children.

A couple enrolled their eleven-year-old son in a private high school because they thought the public schools could not accommodate his needs, even by letting him skip several grades. One mother sent her musically talented children to a private school because students could not accept them; they were called "queer" and "gay" by their peers. Another

71

mother, whose daughter was reading fifth-grade books in kindergarten, says a feeble attempt at a program for the gifted was "just an effort by the board to get us to shut up and go home. We are a minority and they know it."

Joan Smutny, who heads gifted education programs at National College of Education, says, "Some schools just put a gifted child in a corner and give him independent study. That's not enough; he needs to share his ideas with others and to experiment without punishment."[7]

Early identification of the gifted child is important. Some signs to look for are:

- inclination to work independently
- ability to concentrate for long periods of time
- selecting more difficult responses, solutions, or problems in preference to easy or obvious ones
- ability to examine problems critically—not out of contrariness but in trying to understand them
- capacity to generalize
- a developed sense of right and wrong
- sensitivity to others

The type of school program your child needs should include diversified teaching styles and emphasize original thinking, individualized instruction, independent activities, small group discussion, opportunities for research, and a variety of ideas, situations, and experiences. Remember that your child has a right to learn in his own learning style. It is unfair and unfortunate that too often the child who "fits" into a convenient curriculum succeeds scholastically, while the one who wanders from that structure fails.

A parent who knows his child is gifted can follow some of those same guidelines at home. Gifted children must be challenged by activities, people, opportunities, and special projects. The "extras" for the average child are vital to the gifted one—books, lectures, museums, concerts, and social interaction. Give your gifted child room to satisfy his insatiable curiosity and use his inventive imagination.

And don't push too hard. One woman, now fifty-four, was a piano prodigy at the age of four. Her father pushed her into a professional career unrelentingly until, at the age of sixteen, she fled both her father and the piano. Today she is a fine pianist, but she regrets that she was not allowed to develop her skill at a more natural pace.[8]

A gifted child still needs time to grow and absorb life, even if his intellectual abilities are on a fast track.

Busing: obnoxious and ineffective

The issue of busing to achieve racial desegregation in schools has surely been one of the most explosive educational issues in recent decades. According to the Civil Rights Commission, twenty-five years after the Supreme Court outlawed racial segregation in schools, nearly half the 10.5 million black, Hispanic, and other minority students in the United States still attend public schools that are "at least moderately segregated." In the Northeast and North Central regions, two of every three minority students are in partially segregated schools.[9] Busing has been a bitter disappointment.

As whites have fled from large cities, we have seen the urban neighborhood schools disintegrate. In many of the major cities there are so few whites left that no matter how we shuffle students, schools will be predominantly black. In Washington, D.C., the minority school population is 96 percent; in Atlanta, 89 percent; in San Antonio, 85 percent; and in Detroit, 82 percent.[10] David Armor, senior sociologist with the Rand Corporation of Santa Monica, California, claims that "busing, whether voluntary or mandatory, has failed to deliver its promised educational and social benefits. In most desegregated school districts . . . the achievement gap between minority and white students is as large as it was before busing."[11]

I am patently opposed to busing. It hasn't *worked*! Children are uprooted from their neighborhoods, their playmates, and their classmates, and are thrust into unfamiliar and unfriendly environments. Parents are anxious about their children's welfare during the long bus rides.

Education built primarily on racial balance will produce theoretical equality without learning quality. And children have a right to that quality.

Schools were never designed (nor were yellow buses) as agents for desegregation. They are institutions for learning. I believe that parents—minority and majority alike—should have the option of sending their children to schools where they can receive the highest quality education available. If the parents' choice sends a school's racial equilibrium askew, so be it.

Privacy rights—and wrongs

Another issue has stirred heated debate in the courts since the Family Educational Rights and Privacy Act was passed in 1974. The act grants parents (and students over fourteen without parental consent) access to all official records. Information cannot be released to anyone except educational officials without written consent from parents or the student (if he is over eighteen).[12]

The shocking truth, however, is that many schools blatantly violate the intent and the letter of the law by maintaining two sets of files—one for parents and a different one for themselves. One educator said schools use the double file system because they fear confronting parents with the truth about their children.

Schools seem to have no fear when they invade students' lockers or desks. Despite Fourth Amendment protection against unreasonable searches, students' lockers may still be searched by school officials who have a "reasonable suspicion." (Police, on the other hand, must have a search warrant or the student's consent.)

I fully believe a child has as much a right to know about his school records, and as much a right to privacy, as I do. Are we not speaking of the same right that every adult in America takes for granted? If we allow secret files and dramatic, unwarranted invasions of children's property, we leave open the possibility—perhaps the probability—of losing our own rights in this area.

Private schools or none at all?

Given these myriad problems in the public schools, it is only natural that parents and educators are suggesting alternatives.

One such option, the private school movement, is perhaps the fastest growing system of education in America. According to Stanford education professor Michael Kirst, 40 percent of California's residents had children in public schools during the 1950s. Today it is 25 percent—and declining.[13] Many parents are trying to protect children from poor curricula, substandard textbooks, busing, overcrowding, and teachers' strikes by placing them in what they believe to be superior learning environments.

Although I support the right of every parent to send his child to a private school, I believe many such parents are trying to do the right thing the wrong way. Instead of working with the public schools to improve them, they are, as their own kids would say, "copping out." Most private school students are predominantly Northern, white, and wealthy.[14] Does that teach children to interact with other races and cultures? Does that teach children to cope with the unsheltered adult world? I would prefer to see parents work to improve the public system before rejecting it in favor of the private one.

The most dramatic solution to problems in public education is, of course, abolishing compulsory schooling altogether. Proponents argue that more than 10,000 teachers a month are attacked or robbed. If the present rate of vandalism continues, it will cost the public schools of America more than $600 million a year. Nearly 15 percent of the school-age children in our largest cities are almost permanently absent from school, and the figure is high and rising in the suburbs as well.

Dr. Roger Sipher, associate professor of history at the State University of New York at Cortland, argues that eliminating compulsory education "would mean that having a high school diploma would once again be something to be proud of." The move, he says, would permit teachers to concentrate on teaching rather than on discipline, increase public esteem for schools, give renewed meaning to grades, and reduce costs.[15]

Those claims may be valid, but I believe the American educational system, in spite of all its problems, is the mainstay of our social system, not its bane. I have been critical in this chapter because we must face weaknesses before we can correct them. If mandatory education were abolished, I believe we would see rampant intellectual abuse. Those parents who do not adequately *support* the school system now would hardly be able to *replace* it and educate their own children.

Although abolishing compulsory education might solve some learning problems, it would encourage others. Consider the words of Richard Ihle, a Wisconsin high-school teacher.

> My most serious truants, who have regularly slipped through the nets of compulsory education for many years, do not spend the time when they are supposed to be in school working, exploring nature, visiting nursing homes, or painting pictures. They steal, vandalize, smoke pot, insult passersby, and make babies. I have a fear that by lowering the compulsory school age—or eliminating it entirely—we are going to greet our doom like Rome sinking in a sea of barbarians of its own making.[16]

Is there any hope?

Although I have dwelt primarily on the negative in this chapter, I certainly don't want to imply that all schools today are doing a poor job. Scattered across the country are excellent models of schools that approach education in the *right* way. New Trier East High School in Winnetka, Illinois, is an example.

Let me quote for you a part of New Trier's statement of philosophy.

> New Trier's highest aspirations are epitomized in the words on the Dedicatory Plaque, ". . . to commit minds to inquiry, hearts to compassion and lives to the service of mankind." . . . We believe that the most effective instructional program appeals not only to the mind but also to the heart, encouraging and inspiring students to inquire, to evaluate and ulti-

78

mately, on the basis of sound judgment and personal conviction, to act. . . .

We believe that the individual's realization of personal aspirations depends upon the development of self-discipline and social responsibility. Thus, the school community should encourage the development of self-discipline through an environment which provides both the responsibilities and the risks which free people encounter. . . . Our hopes for our students are tempered by our awareness that the heroic and the tragic are inextricably bound together in the human condition.

Those lofty words are not left forgotten in the school's brochures but are actually put into practice. For example, before a student enters New Trier, he is encouraged to attend summer school there to ease the transition to high school. When he begins his freshman year, he is placed in a group of thirty to thirty-five students of the same sex and grade level and is assigned a teacher-advisor. Every morning for four years the student meets with his advisor group, and the same advisor, for twenty minutes. It is a time for discussing minor personal or academic problems before they become major, a time for working through social insecurities or decisions about college.

Advisors make it a point to visit every home—not just the homes of students with problems—and they maintain contact with parents throughout a student's high school career. If discipline problems arise, they are handled by the student's advisor or, if

WHO CONTROLS YOUR CHILD?

they are serious, the chairman of advisors or dean. But, says the New Trier Guide Book, "the school anticipates the full support of the home in all disciplinary action taken."

That full support is evident in everything from parent-teacher conferences to athletic events. I was particularly impressed by the astounding rate of participation—more than 90 percent—in one activity during a student's freshman year. On a particular day, school begins at 3 P.M. instead of 9 A.M. so parents may attend classes with their child. The parents' low absentee rate on that day is a joint product of a school that works to involve parents and parents who make time to take part in their children's education.

New Trier is a community of people who take pride in excellence and young people's development. The pride is unselfish. I've noticed after athletic events how team members can't say enough about how well their friends played. Parents, too, rejoice in the success of their neighbors' children as well as their own.

"A student really can't get lost at New Trier," summed up one mother. "They just care."

I could go on at length about New Trier—about its outstanding teachers, its superior curriculum, its extra-curricular activities, and its varied opportunities for students to grow. I could mention the stellar graduates who still recall fondly their high school days there—Charlton Heston, Ann Margaret, Ralph Bellamy. But the magic of New Trier is in that perfect triangle of cooperation—parents, teachers, and children.

In these first five chapters, we have taken a somewhat grim look at the plight of children in our society. We have looked at those whose parents abuse or neglect them, those who are brought before questionable juvenile authorities, and those who are struggling to deal with today's educational dilemmas. Perhaps these unhappy scenes have led you to conclude, as I have, that the best way to influence your child's destiny is to have a strong hand in guiding it.

PART II

CHAPTER SIX

THE CARE AND MAINTENANCE
OF YOUR CHILD:
FROM CRADLE TO COLLEGE

Parents, I'd like to talk to you as something of a "Dutch uncle" as I guide you through the stages of your child's growth—the trying and joyous years of the emerging adult. I'll give you suggestions about encouraging your child's creativity and, in the chapters ahead, I'll try to help you find a satisfactory answer to that nagging question, "Who controls your child?"

Think back to those nine months of "pre-parenthood." You probably imagined you would be delighted, overjoyed, and overcome with happiness when you finally stepped into your new role. However, reality may find you feeling quite the contrary. You may be overwhelmed and overworked. You may find the task arduous, disappointing, draining, frustrating, demanding, and puzzling. Many adults who begin parenthood with the best of intentions throw their hands up in despair when their children's behavior contradicts all their expectations.

As parents, you have the obligation to feed, clothe, house, and educate your children. Parents are the single most important influence on a child's life. Parents must be arbiters, providers, educators, socializers, supporters, adjudicators, cooks, launderers, and chauffeurs. You must nurture your child through years of physical and emotional growth, at the same time cultivating his innate creativity. It is your job to help shape a confused, dependent child into an independent, mature, responsible adult. That does not mean you will supply all your child's needs, nor that you will be in complete control of his life. Parenting is a give-and-take relationship; you may not even recognize how great a role your children play in "shaping" you as they grow.

So here you are, facing a twenty-year responsibility for the physical, intellectual, social, and emotional growth of another human being—and nobody has told you *how*. You didn't go to college for four years to get a parenting degree. You didn't have to pass an exam certifying you as a bona fide, qualified parent. You never even had a crash course in "Parenthood 101." No wonder you're scared!

As an educator and a father of three, I too have felt the weight of responsibility for my children's lives. It's a shame we have to wait so long to see how they turn out! But although I have worked hard at being a parent, I have not forgotten the joys that cannot be duplicated and the moments I would not have wanted to miss. The "care and maintenance" of your child is life's most bittersweet experience.

Babes in arms

You already know infants need the basics: food, clothing, shelter, lots of holding, cuddling, and hugging. A child needs a warm, loving, nurturing environment that creates a bond between parent and child that can remain strong throughout his lifetime. But your responsibilities to your new baby do not end with the bottle, the diaper, and the goodnight kiss. Infancy is no time to "store" your child away in a crib, thinking that the real work starts later. Your child begins learning from the first day he is born, and you are his finest teacher.

Babies need plenty of simple, colorful crib toys so they have an exciting environment to explore with all their senses. Children must touch, taste, see, and feel to become truly original and creative.[1] Play games such as "peek-a-boo"; talk, laugh, and sing to your child to stimulate language and cognitive development. In a few weeks, your baby should begin to respond to these "song-and-dance routines." By eight months, he should begin to distinguish the mother, or mothering person, from all others.

Of course, every normal baby will fuss and cry as a cue to hunger, tiredness, pain, or other discomfort. You will become a Sherlock Holmes as you try to solve the mystery of baby's tears, and it is not uncommon for parents of infants to feel fear, depression, and frustration.

Be patient. Do not take your frustrations out on your child. Remember, he has no other way to communicate at this age, and he needs your love and understanding.

Reach out

Even though my children are nearly grown, I still make it a habit to do two things every night: I pray with them, and I tuck them into bed, wrapping the comforter around them and making sure they're warm.

The importance of the second point is that we need to touch; whether we're touching people or things, we need that sensory experience. The chance to touch and feel opens the door to a child's creativity as he grows and learns. A baby will touch and taste an item the first time he encounters it because that is his way of processing information. Even older children cannot learn solely from books and must add this "touch" dimension to their learning process.

Homes where children live should not be museums. A friend related the story of an aunt whose living room furniture was always covered with plastic. Her carpet was white, not to be trod upon by tiny feet. Her coffee table was delicate glass, not to be fingerprinted by tiny hands. I don't know whether her son developed his creative powers, but if he did he must have explored someone else's living room.

At the very least, parents should have a safe, "child-proof" room where a youngster is free to explore. Children must be able to pick up objects, to feel them, examine them, experience them firsthand.

Children who learn to use the sense of touch as part of their learning style have an added dimension in their lives. Ask a child who has learned to touch what he thinks of when he hears the word "hard" or "soft" and you'll get answers like these:

—as hard as your mother's voice when she is mad at you

—as soft as your mother's lap

—as soft as kitten's hair

—as soft as a heart

Remember, too, to touch each other. I ache when I see parents who show no signs of affection toward one another. Touching and being touched by those we care for not only breathes life into our senses, but it also makes us feel warm and secure. A popular bumper sticker says, "Have you hugged your kid today?" What better way to say "I love you" than to wrap your child in your arms, to hold him close, and to let him feel that you care? I've always hugged my wife, my kids, and my friends. I don't think hugging is "unmanly" or in poor taste. To me it says, "I like you. I appreciate you. You're important." I communicate with a hug just as I communicate verbally, and a young child needs both.

Do you remember the first word your child spoke? Do you remember all the commotion and praise it triggered? That is the kind of positive reinforcement your child needs as he develops his language skills. Let him know you care about what he wants to say even before he knows exactly how to say it. Talk to him and give him the attention he craves. This will be even more important as your child approaches the next stage of development.

The "terrible twos" and other tales

The preschool years are full of energy—theirs, not necessarily yours. Children will grow out of crib toys and into blocks, sand, clay, puzzles, tricycles, and lots of other toys.

They need toys. Even a bathtub can be turned into

a magic wonderland by adding a finger paint playtime before bath. When the painting session is over, the tub and the child can be washed together. Children need space to run, climb, and explore; they need a chance to touch, feel, smell, hear, and see their world.

You should also talk to your child a great deal during this time, naming things, explaining things. Parents are the catalyst for their children's language development, and language is the key to thinking, learning, and reading. That doesn't mean you should be a walking encyclopedia, speaking in complex sentences.

A friend tells about being cross with her daughter, ending her tirade by telling the child "not to do it again." The child retorted, "I won't, just as soon as I figure out what it is I'm not supposed to do!" Too often we think our message is clear when our children have only heard a barrage of words. Are you just talking, or are you communicating?

Children go through periods of tremendous language growth and learning as they develop a working knowledge of grammar. They learn the regularities, patterns, and rules—not consciously, but implicitly—that make creativity possible. We know the child has learned these rules because he says things he could not have learned from others. When a child has developed a rule, he will generalize it to fit similar situations. So he blurts out "goofs" and "one-liners" in youthful innocence.

Chukovsky cites the classic example of the child who looked at his naked body and announced that he was "barefoot all over." He was extending a concept he knew (barefoot) and applying it to a new situation (a bare body).[2] Piaget, world-renowned psychologist, suggests that children's "errors" are not only clues to their thoughts, but also to changes in intelligence as their minds develop. Do not criticize or overlook your child's language errors; they are a result of what is happening inside.

You can also help your child's language develop by expanding his vocabulary and his sentence structure.[3] If a child says, "Dog, pretty dog," you can say, "Yes, it is a pretty dog. What a pretty brown dog." Explain things: "We can't go to the park because it is raining." Expand curiosity by asking questions like, "What will happen if . . . you put the soap in the water . . . or the boat in the water?"

Point out the relationship of objects, such as large compared to small. Take children on walks through the neighborhood. Describing the parts of a house—garret, gargoyle, shutter, bay window—all help improve vocabulary while giving a mental image of the word's meaning. Even giving examples of double entendres is an excellent method of teaching multiple word meanings. Jokes and riddles are good ways to incorporate current events into language development.

Make language fun. On car trips, have contests to see who can remember riddles and who can repeat tongue twisters. Both parents and children can sharpen their tongues and their wits.

Once upon a time

Another ideal language development tool is storytelling and story reading. Children who listen to stories experience the joy of language that is distinctly absent when they hear only language to get things done by: get up, get dressed, eat your breakfast, wash your hands.

Stories provide a fantasy world, which is far more valuable than textbook facts in helping your child deal with reality. You may be surprised how favorite stories—perhaps the same one told over and over—can motivate children to draw or act out their own interpretations. And when you put children to bed with "once upon a time," you're establishing a warm, comfortable atmosphere they'll always identify with reading. That symbol will be a springboard to creativity and a lifelong appreciation for literature.

Respond to your child's emotional needs during this time by comforting him if he is hurt or distressed. A young child leans heavily on his parents for support. Enjoy your child and spend "special time" together. Be careful about sibling rivalry; it is important for each child to feel you are fair and that you care about him as a person.

It is very easy to play favorites in the family, for you can't (and shouldn't) treat all children alike. But there is a difference between not treating them all alike and being unfair. If it is always the baby's turn to sit next to you in the car, what does that say to the older children? If it is always the older child who gets the new clothes, what does that say to the younger children? It says they must misbehave to get your attention.

You may want to enroll your child in a nursery school to encourage social relationships with peers.

Help your child interpret and understand social situations, such as sharing and taking turns. Handling these situations poorly may cause a child to be isolated by peers who don't want to play with him.

No is a two-letter word

Early childhood is a trying time for parents because a child is striving for independence. A two-letter word—"No!"—will probably be his favorite, and "I can do it myself" will be his battle cry. Believe it or not, this signals a positive stage in his development; when a child fights about toilet training or other situations, he is showing signs of autonomy and eventual independence.

If the parents resort to harsh punishment, the child may respond with passive acquiescence or deviousness. Lying can become an expedient means of avoiding anger and punishment. As one seven-year-old explained, "If I lie and don't get caught, then you aren't angry. If I lie and get caught, you get mad—but you would have gotten mad anyway."

Too much autonomy too soon, however, is not good for preschoolers. Release your children gradually, in measured doses, being sensitive to their ability to take on added responsibility. Many inner-city preschool children are allowed to roam free on the streets with no parental guidance or supervision. I recall one mother who was proud that her three-year-old would leave the house all day and return home at dinner time. This child was later referred to authorities for emotional problems.

As a first step, try letting your child do most of his

93

own dressing and undressing when you think he is ready. Let him know you expect him to pick up his toys after he plays with them. This may mean you will have to help for a while; you cannot expect a perfect cleanup job from a two- or three-year-old. Strike a balance between straightjacket controls and complete freedom of choice. Little things can help, such as giving the child options. Don't ask, "Do you want to go to bed?" Instead, say, "Do you want to wear your blue or yellow pajamas tonight when you go to bed?" He then has the choice, and probably will not fight about bedtime.

If you find yourself constantly punishing, fighting, and battling with your child, look at your own needs, motives, and behaviors. Many parents abandon all controls during this period, thus creating willful, self-centered, "spoiled" children. Find the middle ground.

Winning the primaries

During the primary years, you should begin teaching your child to be responsible by helping with household chores, getting ready for school on time, and doing other jobs. Encourage friendships and hobbies that help him grow intellectually and socially. During this time, your child will begin to talk more and use more complex sentences. Answer his questions when possible; encourage dinner table conversation. Discuss any learning difficulties or other problems, and help him assess situations. He may not understand why he wasn't chosen for the

94

school baseball team or invited to a birthday party. School projects may be troubling him and, despite his increasing independence, he needs your support and help.

More than anything, he needs your ear. I clearly remember one night when our son Mark was small, and I was too wrapped up in work to hear what he considered very important news. Finally he pulled hard on my sleeve and cried, "Daddy, you're not listening to me!"

He was right.

Like many parents, I had blocked out this bit of "interference." We learn the skill early. Our society presents such a barrage of sounds—people talking, horns honking, phones ringing, typewriters clacking—that we tune them out. But if you tune out your children when they're young, you'll turn off their creativity.

It isn't easy. Listening takes time, patience, and understanding. Research shows that we listen only ten seconds of every minute someone talks.

With children, I have found it easier to listen at the close of the day than at the beginning, when they're charged with energy and eager to be unleashed. Plan some private time with your child at night and take the time to ask, "What happened today?" You need to hear the trivia as well as the "earthshaking" events. I've always taken my kids for rides in the car. I have them alone and they have me alone. That is our time exclusively. The mere fact that we're together is a form of listening, even if we don't speak a word.

Get away

You can also share the wonder of nature with your children. No matter how deeply you're submerged in the asphalt jungle of the city, you can still take your kids away—to a park, a forest preserve, or a garden. They'll discover for themselves the difference between the handiwork of God and the handiwork of man. They'll hold their breath to hear the sounds of leaves rustling or to watch a squirrel scampering up a tree. A five-year-old boy from National College of Education's Demonstration School recently joined his peers on a class outing in the woods. Suddenly he commanded the entourage to stop. "Wait!" he shouted. "I can hear the wind!"

Sharing your child's response to nature is one of the finest ways you can stimulate his creativity. Observing flowers, trees, and animals—really seeing them—is rejuvenating too. Nothing can duplicate the growing tree or the rose that awakens in the morning. Watch your child as you hike in the woods. The four-year-old will see the ant when you see only the anthill.

Buy creative toys

It's a mistake to buy children every sophisticated toy on the market. In terms of creativity, today's toys are mostly useless. How many times have we seen children have more fun with the cardboard box than with the expensive, battery-powered toy that came inside? A doll that crawls, moves, cries, and turns over by itself leaves nothing to the imagination.

A child needs toys that can be many things. Blocks, for example, can be a road, a town, a dollhouse, a bed, chairs. We don't need to buy—in fact, we shouldn't buy—preconstructed towns, fully assembled spaceships, and firehouses complete with trucks and hoses. We're stifling a child's creativity by reinforcing the concept that everything has only one possible use. One toy manufacturer said if he could invent a toy with one tenth the potential for creative play as sand or water, he would be staggeringly wealthy.

Go out and play!

The importance of play has been recognized for centuries. Plato referred to games as children's own devising of a situation. Aristotle referred to the use of play as an outlet for energy. Cominius devised the first puzzle. Anna Freud stated that play is to the child as work is to the adult. Marbles and dishes have been found in Egyptian tombs. Toys have been found at American Indian sites.

Clare Cherry, in tracing the history of toys, concluded that the number and types of toys used in a society are proportional to the complexity of the society, as well as to its prosperity.[4] Games such as hide-and-seek, kite flying, and card games have been part of children's play for centuries. "Play is the child's way of coping with life," Cherry says. A child is able to deal with the problems as well as the stresses of life through play. It is a vehicle through which children can invent new and wonderful worlds.

Have you ever watched monkeys or chimps in the zoo? They allow and encourage their young to play with each other, with their parents, and with other materials, such as banana leaves and sticks. Burton White, an eminent authority in parent education, emphasizes that the early play of a parent with the child is crucial to the child's later play. It is only at the age of two and three that a child should play on his own. Before that, he needs his parents to help him learn, to help him master anxiety, and to show him how to receive and give pleasure.

Play enables a child to develop the creative and imaginative side of his character. And play is not *just* play; it is the work of growing and learning and being. Philosopher John Locke wrote nearly three hundred years ago, "Children must not be hindered from being children. . . . They love to be busy; change and variety are what delight them . . . curiosity is but an appetite for knowledge, the instrument nature has provided to remove ignorance."

Adolescence: crayons to Clearasil

If you think parenting is a rocky road when your child is small, brace yourself for adolescence. The most important thing to remember during these tense and emotional years is to keep lines of communication open. Adolescents feel a strong need for independence, but that is not your signal to withdraw guidance and support. If you think you are baffled and frustrated, just remember that adolescents are often just as bewildered about their own behavior and volatile, sometimes uncontrollable, emotions. The adolescent faces the perilous pitfalls of drugs, alcohol, and promiscuous sex. His body is growing in spurts and is not necessarily in sync with his mind. He's wavering between Saturday morning cartoons and *Saturday Night Fever.*

Again, a balance between giving support and allowing independence is critical. Don't take a stand or fight about everything. Be aware of the child's struggle for identity and the need to "prove" himself grown up. Be conscious of his need to fit in and become a member of a peer group. Encourage proper behavior and friendships; expect unpredictability, sensitivity, overreactions, sullenness, and even insults as he tries to free himself from adult domination. Keep your sense of humor, and don't let your frustration turn into hostility.

"Fishing line philosophy"

Particularly with adolescent children, I follow what I call the "fishing line philosophy" of parenting: I throw out the line, but I reel it back in if I see my children overstepping their limits.

A parent should not abrogate the responsibility of guiding a child during his growing years. A child who is given too much responsibility too soon will experience constant failure; he may see his mother and father as indifferent and uncaring. Children cannot rear themselves. They are not pint-sized adults. They have a right to learn slowly, to make mistakes.

Likewise, a child cannot be given responsibility so late that he has no opportunity to practice for the future. He must not be reared in an environment so tightly structured that when he finally breaks away from home he becomes the antithesis of his parents' design.

Many parents cannot seem to operate on a level of trust, so they substitute structure. They become guards instead of guardians. They do not communicate to their children what is expected of them, why it is expected, and how important certain roles are in the family. I believe in being authoritative, not authoritarian, as you'll see in a later chapter on obedience and respect. But most of all, I believe we must help children learn and grow.

If it is not already one of your good habits, I hope that very soon you will take the time to talk to your child. Don't leave the knowledge you may have gained from this chapter on deposit in your head. Act. Communicate your love to your child.

CHAPTER SEVEN

CHILDREN AND TELEVISION: TUNED IN OR TURNED OFF?

Jeffrey is a five-year-old hurricane, awhirl in a violent fantasy. His teachers cannot tame him. They describe him as "having trouble standing still, having little or no attention and interest span, hard to manage, naughty, a discipline problem, very aggressive, and always at battle with his sister and brother." You see, reality for Jeffrey is guns, monsters, spaceships, and the *Six-Million Dollar Man.*[1]

Two thirteen-year-olds and a twelve-year-old in Miami were charged with first-degree murder after pouring gasoline over a woman and setting her afire. They were mimicking a scene from a television movie.[2]

These situations are dramatic, but not surprising. A child graduating from high school today will have viewed an estimated 15,000 hours of television— 4,000 more hours than he will have spent in school—according to the Nielsen Index figures for TV viewing.[3] He will have witnessed some 40,000 acts of violence, more than a third of which were murders.[4] In the course of a year, the average

WHO CONTROLS YOUR CHILD?

American child spends more time watching TV than doing anything else but sleeping. Even a six-month-old infant is already stimulated by television more than one hour a day.

It is no wonder that television is being recognized as a major influence on children, right alongside—and perhaps stronger than—the family, the school, peers, and the church. TV has become a third parent . . . or the only parent. It is a tremendously effective teacher, loyal buddy, and bottomless pit of entertainment.

Something is wrong here. We have let a small screen with moving pictures take control of our children. When someone asks, "Do you know where your children are?" we congratulate ourselves if they are "safely" checked—like a coat—in front of the "boob tube." People, we are fooling ourselves! Although the research on television's effects is contradictory, I believe our children are not at all safe from stifled imagination, cultural deprivation, lethargy, boredom, reduced language skills, poor reading ability, and exaggerated expectations.

We have seen this phenomenon only since we have gone from being a nation with a chicken in every pot to one with a TV in every living room. Nearly every American home has at least one television set, and many have two. When Ed Sullivan and *I Love Lucy* replaced radio's *Shadow*, researchers rushed to document TV's grasp on our youth. However, early studies concluded that although television had become a permanent family member, its effects on preschool and primary students were positive.[5]

Negative effects were seen, however, with ten- to thirteen-year-olds, who seemed to reach a saturation point where knowledge drops as TV watching rises.[6]

Today, "progress" has given researchers new factors to investigate—the possible link between TV violence and aggressive behavior, and the influence of Madison Avenue on wide-eyed young viewers. The questions continue to be batted back and forth. Are kids slaves to TV? Dr. Daniel R. Anderson of the University of Massachusetts in Amherst thinks not. His National Science Foundation study says a child who appears "glued to the tube" hasn't been enslaved by the video monster; his problems probably lie elsewhere—in his home life, relationships, or at school.[7]

I am in somewhat of a quandary. On one hand, I don't believe in tossing the television into the trash, as one respected educator and close friend of mine has done. To completely deny children the pleasures of television is to magnify its fascination. On the other hand, there is much frightening evidence about television's influence that is too devastating to ignore.

Drugged by the tube

Children are bored. To me, this is incredible. There is so much in this world to see and do that I have never understood how adults could be bored, much less children. But teachers today say kids come to school exhausted—not from climbing for hours on a jungle gym or playing tag in the alley or baseball in the park. Instead, their energy has been sapped by *Barney Miller, Buck Rogers,* and *Three's Company.*

Researcher Nancy Larrick, writing in *Learning Magazine,* says teachers also report shorter attention spans now than in years past. Eight or ten minutes seems to be the longest time children can work on a task. After tuning in all night, they tune out in class and can't seem to focus on lessons. I do not lay the entire blame on television; I am sure that the poor quality of classroom teaching in many schools and the increasing rate of teacher "burnout" are contributing factors. But television still appears to be the primary culprit.

Today, the motto of "If at first you don't succeed, try, try again" is lost on children. Students toss unfinished pictures or stories in the wastebasket after one or two attempts. They seem to expect instant success and immediate rewards. Persistence is not on their frequency; they would rather be entertained than create. Lethargy is indeed an epidemic when "energetic" youth like the sixth graders in an affluent New York community are found sitting on the curb waiting for recess to end.[8]

Furthermore, these children, mesmerized by situation comedies and space adventures, are forming distorted pictures of reality in their minds. They experience life, observes Kenneth Keniston, chairman and director of the Carnegie Council on Children, "as a series of quick takes, constant excitement, incessant movements, instant resolutions."[9]

Those of us who still remember how vividly we "saw" the *Green Hornet* and *Inner Sanctum* on radio should be outraged when we see television stonewalling our children's imagination. The stories they write in school are mere regurgitations of the plots and reiterations of the same dialog they heard the night before.

In some ways, five-year-olds are as "aged" as the stereotypical couple seated each night before what one author calls "the plug-in drug."[10] In some cases, kindergarten children must be *taught* how to play! We can no longer assume that two children know how to roll a ball back and forth, although we can assume they know how to turn on a television set.[11]

Dorothy G. Singer, co-director of the Family Television Research Consultation Center, Yale University, reports that the children who watch the least amount of television and who engage in make-believe play are the most imaginative, cooperative, persistent, and joyful. They also have more imaginary companions than children who are heavy television viewers.[12]

Not only may children's imaginations suffer, but they may also have trouble distinguishing between reality and fantasy. They are at a gullible, susceptible age. They're not yet sure about right and wrong, and we cannot expect them to sort out fake from fact.

I predict that the children of today who list television as their hobby will be the listless retirees of tomorrow. It is appalling to hear teachers say that model airplanes, butterfly collections, and toy railroads lure few youngsters. They sit and stare, waiting for someone to change the channel on life's television set. What will these children expect as adults? Where will their motivation for achievement, for betterment come from? How will they manifest their disillusionment when their "plot" turns sour and there is no "off" button?

Perhaps they'll shrug their shoulders or punch someone in the nose. There is some evidence that body language may replace verbal skills for video-addicted children. They spend little time talking to their parents or peers. They get little practice in expressing themselves.[13] So if words don't come easily, they give us an instant replay of what they have heard from television heroes.

A further danger of excessive TV watching follows logically—and dismally. Children are losing their desire and ability to read. When we read we create our own images; television delivers them prepackaged. Says psychologist Bruno Bettelheim, "Television captures the imagination but does not liberate it. A good book at once stimulates and frees the mind."[14]

Reading militates against passivity. When you read you are in control. The lazy TV viewer is often reluctant to become a thoughtful reader. This comment came from the twelve-year-old daughter of a college English teacher:

> I mean television, you don't have to worry about getting really bored because it's happening and you don't have to do any work to see it, to have it happen. But you have to work to read, and that's no fun. I mean it's fun when it's a good book, but how can you tell if the book will be good? Anyhow, I'd rather see it as a television program.[15]

Children with reading problems are hurt the most. According to Marie Winn, author of *The Plug-In Drug*, "Television plays a profoundly negative role in such children's intellectual development, since it is only by reading a great deal that they can hope to overcome their reading problems."[16]

And now, a word about the sponsors . . .

Perhaps the harshest criticism of television in relation to children is directed at commercials—and justifiably so. The United States is one of only three countries worldwide that allow commercials on children's television programs.[17] A child under twelve may see 25,000 commercials in a year,[18] blaring messages that urge him to buy or beg for sugar-laden cereals, tasty candy bars, new games, and exotic toys his parents may not want him to have and may not be able to afford. A young child will have a hard time resisting seasoned writers, producers, directors, musicians, and artists skilled in the powers of persuasion.

Consumer advocate Robert Choate, testifying in Senate hearings, said, "In the 1930s a mother . . . fended off aggressive door-to-door salesmen eager to get junior's ear. Today she is told to protect the innocent while 22 salesmen per hour beseech her child over the tube, disguised as the friendly folk of cartoon, jingle and adventureland."[19] The number of commercials per hour now averages eighteen to twenty, but the blatant and subliminal messages continue to ensnare gullible youth.

WHO CONTROLS YOUR CHILD?

Researchers point out three major concerns about TV advertising aimed at young people:

- Children's reasoning powers are not fully developed; thus, they cannot properly evaluate sales messages.
- Commercials stress brand differences and materialism, rather than moral and ethical values.
- The reality of the product when obtained may be far less exciting than the commercials promised. Therefore, a child may become cynical about other sources of information and authority.[20]

Commercials pay the bills for television programs. And some people have charged that programs are shaped by people who are more interested in their bank accounts than in children's welfare.

I support the right of cereal manufacturers, toy makers, and others to advertise. I believe in the free enterprise system, and I encourage promotion. In my experience with hundreds of business leaders, seldom have I encountered a lack of concern and sensitivity for children and families. But I believe that many businessmen become trapped in marketing programs inconsistent with their personal values. Therein lies the real crime. The person who knowingly promotes a product in a way that is clearly in violation of children's rights commits an injustice both upon himself and upon the children who see and hear his promotion.

CHILDREN AND TELEVISION

TV: a family matter

Commercials' exaggerated claims and their insistent urge to "buy, buy, buy" are often the basis for parent-child conflict. Children think they cannot live without the latest *Star Wars* toy or game, and the parent becomes the villain if he forbids the dream toy. Excessive materialism is not among the values most parents want to teach their children, yet that's the message commercials convey. Children are convinced that a product must be good when they hear the hard sell of charismatic super-personalities they admire. While an athlete on the tube is extolling the virtues of a new candy bar, Mother or Father is in the kitchen trying to convince a child to eat an apple. All in all, commercials create a world that is unreal, unwholesome, and unfit for our children.

My children were no different from yours. They wanted "junk food" and the glittery, heavily hyped toys. But I didn't stop them from watching television commercials. Rather, I fought advertisers with the best weapon any parent has—education. The combination of school lessons about good nutrition and the examples my wife and I set enabled our children to decide for themselves what kinds of foods they should eat, and their decisions were sound.

When it came to toys, I was highly selective in what I permitted them to have. I am by no means saying that my skills of persuasion were an instant success. I must admit that at times I felt my reasoning powers were no match for the slick promoters; it would have been much easier to give in and buy the toys or the sugary cereals. But I was not ready to relinquish my responsibilities—and my rights—as a parent to counterbalance TV's magnetism.

Television is an interloper that can violate not only parents' rights or children's rights, but family rights—if you let it.

"The primary danger of the television screen," psychologist Urie Bronfenbrenner has said, "lies not so much in the behavior it produces as in the behavior it prevents—the talks, the games, the family activities and the arguments through which much of the child's learning takes place and his (or her) character is formed."[21] Today we must strive even harder to keep the family unit intact, as forces even more powerful than television threaten to drive a wedge between generations.

Teachers tell us that children today are lonely;[22] when they come home from school they are greeted not by a smiling mother with milk and warm chocolate chip cookies, but by reruns of *I Dream of Jeannie*. Captain Kangaroo sends them off to school in the morning and *Laverne and Shirley* or the *Incredible Hulk* puts them to bed. Television is parent, pal, confidant, and dinner companion. *The Waltons* may be the only family many children share dinner with.

"In some households members of a family may never utter a word to each other for days, because most of their free time is spent communicating with the characters on the TV screen. They move through the house as strangers. Or if there is verbal communication it may be in the form of an incomplete sentence, sounding like a semi groan or grunt," writes Nat Rutstein in *Go Watch TV!*[23]

A parent or other family member's attempt to start a conversation in the midst of a program may be rebuffed. A grandmother described her feelings: "Sometimes when I come to visit the girls I'll walk into their room and they're watching a TV program. Well, I know they love me, but it makes me feel bad when I tell them hello, and they say, without even looking up, 'Wait a minute . . . we have to see the end of this program.' It hurts me to have them care more about that machine and those little pictures than about being glad to see me. I know that they probably can't help it, but still. . . ."[24]

In many other countries the situation is the same. Argentine families seldom eat a meal without watching television. The chancellor of West Germany once proposed that television programs be cancelled one day a week so that family conversation might be revived. Citizen protest overruled his suggestion.[25]

Some successful efforts have been made to reduce television viewing in the home. At Kimberton Farms, a private school near Phoenixville, Pennsylvania, parents were asked to ban TV viewing by children under eight and to limit it for older children to Friday night through Sunday afternoon. Children on this TV "diet" appeared relaxed, more imaginative, and more innovative.[26]

Television can be an asset when used properly. Some teachers are telling students to watch certain television programs as homework assignments.

They use TV as a resource to teach language arts, social studies, science, and math skills. Programs like *Little House on the Prairie* contain lessons about the westward movement in the United States; *Mork and Mindy* gives food for thought about other cultures, economics, and technology. Programs like *Sesame Street*, the *Electric Company*, and many of those on public television stations also get high marks from me, along with *60 Minutes* and similar news programs.

Some suggested antidotes

1. If you are uneasy about the amount and types of television programs your children are watching, begin planning your "withdrawal" strategy by watching some TV yourself. Set aside time to see what your children are viewing, beginning with Saturday morning cartoons for younger children. (Some cartoons are quite good and teach important lessons about human behavior and acceptance.) Then make a commitment to become involved in the programming of your children's television watching, instead of letting *Charlie's Angels* program you.

2. Carefully select what you consider worthwhile programs and watch them as a family. Discuss them. Explain why certain situations occurred and what lessons might be learned.

3. Provide alternatives. In our home, one night each week is always family night. It's a night of what I call "creative dependence"—we depend on each other to create an evening's entertainment. Family nights show children that you value this

time together as a unit. Besides, down deep, kids would much rather have us than a television set.

4. Set boundaries for TV watching. Unlimited TV privileges are not in the child's best interests. Don't permit kids to watch the tube for endless stretches. Prohibit programs that emphasize violence or reinforce ethnic prejudices.

5. Restrict your own television watching. "Do as I say, not as I do" has never been a sound parenting philosophy. Ask yourself if indeed *you* are a TV addict. How influenced are you by TV programs and commercials? To what lengths will you go to avoid missing *The Edge of Night* or *The Young and the Restless*? (A major religious radio station in Chicago regularly receives prayer requests from listeners worried about their favorite soap opera characters.)

All in all, I favor the format of public television, in which commercial messages are reserved for the end or the beginning of a program. Otherwise, children are trapped into watching the ads, and they will be subjected to the brainwashing techniques of sophisticated video salesmen. Don't be surprised if a child who can't yet see over your kneecaps tells you that when he's out of Schlitz he's out of beer, or that Coke adds life.

CHAPTER EIGHT

RELIGIOUS CULTS: OPIATE OF THE CHILDREN

Steven was one of the smartest students in his high-school class. He cared little for studying, though, and preferred his own company to anyone else's. After many years as an Army "brat," he had attended more schools and severed more friendships than he could count.

One fine day, when Steven was a junior, he jumped on his motorcycle and headed for California. His classmates later learned he had joined the Children of God. His parents have yet to understand why.

Permit me to suggest why. Inside young people like Steven is a void, a spiritual chasm, they yearn to fill with a higher purpose, a meaning that will let them transcend everyday life. Many have found that purpose—and I count myself among them. But in the past twenty years I have seen hundreds of children go desperately astray trying to find it. They are the morally starved who seek to satisfy their appetites by joining fanatical cults.

Despite the Jonestown massacre and the Manson

family slaughters, cults continue to grow. I have included a brief discussion of cults in this book because I believe they point to a spiritual vacuum in our society today and represent an evil force that affects millions of children. We cannot ignore the cults, for they are robbing children and parents of their rights every day, everywhere, with horrifying success.

Who are they and what do they want?

There may be as many as three thousand different cults, representing two to ten million people, in existence today.[1] The definition of what constitutes a cult is an issue wide open to individual interpretation and judgment. My personal definition would include any group or movement that steps outside of the orthodox biblical faith of the historic church, but in this discussion I have in mind primarily the new extremist groups whose charismatic leaders consume the lives of their members. "These cults are 'one-man shows,'" writes Dr. Jack Sparks in *The Mindbenders*, perhaps the best book on current cults from a Christian perspective. "The authority for their authenticity goes back no farther than their founders."[2]

I speak of men like the Rev. Sun Myung Moon and his followers (The Unification Church or "Moonies"), Guru Maharaj Ji (Divine Light Mission), and the late Rev. Jim Jones, whose nine hundred mindless devotees committed mass suicide at the People's Temple commune in Jonestown, Guyana, in 1978. I speak of those who use high-pressure indoctrination, sophisticated psychological coercion, and emotional abuse to divert the young and confused from reality and force them to resign their will.

"Cult recruitment relies on deception," says Louis Jolyon West, M.D., director of U.C.L.A.'s Neuropsychiatric Institute. He adds that recruiters use intimate eye contact and excessive friendliness, at the same time concealing the identity of their group. "A straightforward approach to recruitment would be highly unsuccessful," West says, "For example, 'Hi, I'm John Doe from the Unification Church and I'm talking to you right now because we need more members. We want you to join us, work for us, and turn over all your earnings to our leader, Rev. Moon.' "[3] Few would respond to that invitation.

According to psychologist Margaret Thaler Singer, the cults' methods "amount to conditioning techniques that constrict attention, limit personal relationships, and devalue reasoning." There is "constant exhortation and training to arrive at exalted spiritual states, altered consciousness, and automatic submission to directives; there are long hours of prayer, chanting, or meditation . . . and lengthy repetitive lectures day and night."[4] Family, friends, and proper sexual activity are forbidden in many cases.

The cults' beliefs cover a broad spectrum and are probably the least of the reasons why young people join. The followers of Guru Maharaj Ji, leader of the Divine Light Mission, believe Jesus was the Perfect Master of His time but that Ji has replaced Him. The doctrine of the Moonies says man's physical redemption will happen through a second Messiah, whom they imply is Moon. The Children of God began as a fundamentalist counterculture ministry; now it incorporates the occult, reincarnation, and sexual permissiveness. Followers believe leader David (Moses David) Brandt Berg is the only end-time prophet.[5]

I have seen students give their entire savings to these causes. Members of the Children of God turn over all their money to the leaders. The Rev. Moon, according to *Newsweek*, has bought a divine estate in Frankfurt, Germany, that is reportedly worth $400,000.[6] Cults often assign members to fill daily quotas of $100 to $150 through street sales. Individual members have claimed to raise as much as $1,500 day after day by selling flowers and candy, and by begging.[7] On street corners they cry for money, but inside they cry for answers.

"Spiritual supermarket"

People are looking for simple solutions to complex problems. Young people captured by the cults' spell seek a peaceful way out of their inner turmoil. A study of the Moonies by Marc Galanter and several colleagues of the Albert Einstein College of Medicine in New York showed 39 percent had "serious emotional problems" before their conversion (6 percent had been hospitalized) and 23 percent had a serious drug problem. Also, 91 percent were unmarried, 89 percent were white, 58 percent had been in college before conversion, and 25 percent had

117

completed college.[8] Children join cults because they sense that life is meaningless, and they think cults can provide them with a reason for existence.

Says Singer: "Cults supply ready-made friendships, and ready-made decisions about careers, dating, sex, and marriage, and they outline a clear 'meaning of life.' "[9] British researcher Carol Williams calls cults "a spiritual supermarket ... for people seeking spiritual fitness the way they seek physical fitness."[10]

In my experience as a counselor and an educator, I have seen bright college students drawn by cultists' slick powers of persuasion. I have seen them confused and brainwashed to the point of no return. I have been amazed at how ill-equipped these students were to combat this deadly force. They had no foundation from which to evaluate what was happening; they had no reservoir of values from which to draw strength. Sons and daughters from the best homes—children of doctors, ministers, educators, and business executives—have been unable to resist the magnetism of the cults' promises.

The memory of their vacant stares still chills my marrow. Their conversations were coldly detached, their allegiance alarmingly steadfast. These young people were looking desperately for lasting relationships, no matter how distorted or irrational. For them, it was their way of surviving.

One former member of the Children of God put it this way: "I guess the main reason I joined can be summed up in one word. Bitterness. I had become bitter in my heart. I had seen some genuine shortcomings in the organized church, in the church's lack of ability to reach young people, and then I took it upon myself to become personally offended by this. And you know bitterness leads to rebellion. And rebellion leads to deception."[11]

Rabbi James Rudin and his wife, coauthors of *Prison or Paradise? The New Religious Cults*, profiles the type of person most defenseless against the cults.

The most vulnerable target group for cult recruitment is the person, young or old, who has made no meaningful spiritual connection with an established religion, who is in search of spiritual values and transcendent meaning, who is willing, even yearning for strict discipline and authority, and who may be burdened with guilt about affluence or sex or drugs.

Such a person may enthusiastically make the sacrifices necessary to maintain the love of the cult leader and of his peers within the group. In an age of dislocation, when everything and everyone seems rootless and in flux, when one's own family is seen as superficial and vapid, one's own religion as irrelevant and relativistic, and society as chaotic and uncaring, the absolute claims, guarantees, and promises of cult life are appealing.[12]

Morality begins at home

It is my opinion that in one sense we are all to blame for the proliferation of cults. All of us—if even by our silence or apathy—are reaping what we have sown in today's society, and we are now witnessing a near total moral eclipse.

WHO CONTROLS YOUR CHILD?

I believe that morally and spiritually developed people do not seek out cults. Parents have given over the control of their children to outside influences, while they themselves have become mired in moneymaking, career-advancing, and status-seeking. The video age has programmed children into being spectating robots who lack self-help and decision-making skills. The church is, in many cases, a sanctuary for grown-ups, not for those who are growing up.

Dr. Robert Coles, research psychiatrist for Harvard University Health Services and a perceptive student of children's crises, says society today does not sufficiently emphasize "a child's struggle to make sense of the world and to come to some kind of moral judgment of the way the world works." He says children today "have lost everything except preoccupation with themselves, and this is enhanced every day by the way they are brought up."[13]

I will say it again: Responsibility rests with the parents. Morality begins at home. How many of you parents are listening to your neighbors' problems while your children's inner puzzles are in pieces? I know children of pastors who have joined cults because the pastors ministered only to their congregations and neglected their own families. Coles says parents have surrendered their moral authority to the "experts," to "newspaper columnists who give advice ad nauseam," and to "fads and secular authorities."[14]

And when our homes are dens of cynicism and criticism for the boss, the teacher, the president, the governor, children come to believe the good and the positive can only be had through escape to drugs, alcohol, or wild religions.

Let me encourage you to do something old fashioned. Join with me and so many others today who are admitting they need more than just "the good life." Come back to a personal faith and trust in Jesus Christ as your Lord and Savior. Instill a living faith in Him in your children, and bring them with you to church again. I believe a child's spiritual development is one area in which a parent must be both directive and protective. Too many children are going to hell with our blessing. As the writer of Proverbs said so very well, "Train up a child in the way he should go: and when he is old, he will not depart from it" (Prov. 22:6). We cannot let young people play religious roulette; the odds are too great that they will grow up to be Moonies and Hare Krishnas.

Choose a church that makes the gospel relevant to the conflicts your children face. In many cases, organized religion has overlooked children's needs. Said one theologian, "Traditional religion was so sure of its influence that it didn't realize all these movements fomenting underground were offering something quite similar."[15] Too many churches put their money into buildings instead of into people; they spend millions of dollars for stone or glass cathedrals but not a fraction as much on solid Sunday school literature. The most beautiful sanctuary will not keep a child from another Jonestown. To those who were desperate, Guyana was paradise.

Coming home

We may argue all we want that children have a right to join a cult—and technically they probably do—but they also have a right to leave. And I believe their parents have a right to try to free them. Not surprisingly, the cults fight those rights and have taken anticultists and "deprogrammers" to court. "Stealing" a child from a cult can be viewed as kidnapping. Professional deprogrammers have been accused of psychological warfare and Gestapo techniques as deplorable as those used by cult recruiters. But since few cult members leave on their own, what can parents do?

First, you must deal with your guilt. Realize that you may have made some mistakes in the past, but don't wallow in them. Admit what has happened and seek help from countercult organizations* and a lawyer.[16] Try to understand what has happened, and learn the facts about the cult to which your child belongs. Talk to parents who are or have been in your situation. Keep open the lines of communication and love between you and your child at all times. Don't be afraid to talk to him on a spiritual level; that is his current frame of reference. Above all, don't ever disown him no matter what his behavior.

---

*Countercult groups include the American Family Foundation in Lexington, Massachusetts, the Citizens' Freedom Foundation in Redondo Beach, California, and others.

RELIGIOUS CULTS: OPIATE OF THE CHILDREN

All these factors will be important when your child reenters society. In many ways he will be like a prisoner of war coming home, permanently scarred mentally and emotionally. He may never be what he was before, but he can recapture reality. Singer says it takes eight to eighteen months for a former cultist "to become a fully functional member of mainstream society." She notes that they face six key problems: "floating," or the tendency to slip into altered states of consciousness; loneliness; problems in decision-making; depression; guilt and difficulty dealing with those still in the cult; reentry into their family and the outside world. Listen to these former cultists.

I come in and can't decide whether to clean the place, make the bed, cook, sleep, or what. I just can't decide about anything and I sleep instead. I don't even know what to cook. The group used to reward me with candy and sugar when I was good. Now I'm ruining my teeth by just eating candy bars and cake.

Weeks after I left, I would suddenly feel spacy and hear the cult leader saying, "You'll always come back. You are one with us. You can never separate." I'd forget where I was, that I'm out now; I'd feel his presence and hear his voice. I got so frightened once that I slapped my face to make it stop.

I borrowed my dad's car to drive about 65 miles out into the country and help this guy I had just met once in a coffeehouse to transport some stolen merchandise because he spoke in such a strong and authoritative way to me on the phone. I can't believe how much I still obey people.[17]

Singer says all but five of the more than three hundred former cultists she has treated have resumed careers or returned to school. (The five joined nonresidential cults.) Some who are deprogrammed, however, return again. One woman, baptized in the Disciples of Christ as a youth, became a Moonie, was deprogrammed and became an ardent anti-cultist, and then reconverted.[18]

How can society help?

We face in this country the dilemma of controlling cults without stifling the First Amendment. One lawyer who has been involved in many cult cases on the "anti" side said: "I don't accept the proposition that merely because you call yourself a religion that you are suddenly cloaked in the protection of the First Amendment."[19] In contrast, Stephen Chapman, writing in *The New Republic*, says a recent cult hearing conducted by Senator Robert Dole was "a reminder of how fragile and precarious the First Amendment's protections are. It was also a reminder that anyone who doesn't believe the First Amendment protects the liberties of Moonies doesn't believe in the First Amendment."[20]

I fully respect the First Amendment. But I also believe cults have been given too many freedoms that infringe on others' rights. As the saying goes, "Your rights end where my nose begins." If a person does not have the right to falsely yell "fire" in a crowded theater, neither do cultists have the right to harass airport travelers and unsuspecting children. We are dealing with more than a public nuisance.

RELIGIOUS CULTS: OPIATE OF THE CHILDREN

We are dealing with forces beyond human rationality, merchants of destruction who cannot be allowed to control our children.

Let me suggest four specific steps you, your church, and your community can take to protect our freedom from the cults.

1. Bring moral and spiritual instruction back into your home. Open up with your children; talk to them about knowing Christ. Ask your pastor for some good Bible study literature. At our house, we've found that five- to ten-minute times of Scripture reading and prayer at mealtime are far more effective than trying for twenty or thirty minutes. I would rather have them wanting more than to risk overstuffing them beyond their capacity to learn.

2. Work together in your community for the licensing of cult recruiters. It's time we resist making our people prey to these anonymous charlatans.

3. Call for ordinances to keep religious pests (of *all* kinds) from cruising our airports and shopping malls at will. The print media, the radio, and the TV are all means of communication of religious messages, and I'm for giving all people, most notably our children, a bit of a reprieve from such messages as they shop or hurry to a plane.

4. Finally, it is time for cult education both in the church and in the home. More and more churches are undertaking various instructional series on

the cults—especially the newer cults. Not only is this helpful, but follow-up discussions add to our education. (Several of the articles in this book's bibliography will prove helpful here.)

We must do all of this—and more—to stop the cults. What our children seek is justifiable; what they get from these insidious zealots is unforgivable. And what they really need are committed Christian mothers and fathers to lead and love them.

CHAPTER NINE

HONOR THY CHILDREN: OBEDIENCE, DISCIPLINE, AND RESPECT

"Honor thy father and mother." I believe in that scriptural passage. I also believe in its corollary: Honor thy children. It's easy to forget that phrase as our tame, adoring, trusting babies erupt into unpredictable, temperamental, and often rebellious human beings. But misbehavior is a part of growing up, a part of separating right from wrong, of searching for black-and-white answers in a mixed-up world shaded mostly in gray.

Obedience and discipline rarely have been problems in our home. I believe informed obedience—spelling out the rules clearly and sticking to them—creates respect and eliminates major discipline problems. But every child will misbehave at one time or another, and it may be a comfort to know that he has his reasons. You are not necessarily a rotten parent, and you probably don't have rotten kids.

Why they're misbehavin'

In his book *Children: The Challenge*,[1] child psychologist Rudolph Dreikurs points out four major trouble spots that cause a child to misbehave. You will recognize them all.

1. *Attention-getting.* A little girl gleefully skips into the kitchen, bubbling with pride over having done the shopping. The attention she gets is her mother's stern comment, "I hope you got everything." An overjoyed boy flies into the house, shouting, "I got a hundred on my test!" His father replies, "How many times have I told you not to slam the door?"

Did you feel a pang of guilt as you read these examples? How often have you been too busy cooking dinner, reading the newspaper, watching television, burying your nose in office work, or talking with friends to pay attention to your own children? A child who is repeatedly ignored by his parents will soon decide that negative attention is better than none at all, and he will try every way he knows to become the focal point of family life. If the news of a superior test grade won't coax you from your bridge game, a bottle of grape juice spilled on the new sofa undoubtedly will.

2. *Power.* Kids learn how to get it and use it early. The following grocery store scene is repeated daily across our country. Tommy grabs some candy off the shelf. Mother tells him no. Tommy screams and kicks and cries, drawing scowls from passing shoppers and a few sympathetic looks for Tommy's mother. Mother either backs down, sighing, as Tommy's tears instantly dry and he stuffs the

candy in his mouth; or she holds firm, resorting to a good thwacking right there in the aisle. Either way, Tommy gets the upper hand.

There will be those times, too, when nothing you do is right. You will be the constant object of judgment, criticism, and ridicule. ("Oh, Mother! How could you wear *that!*" or "*Nobody* says *that* any more!") You will be blamed for what you are and for what you do. Oscar Wilde wrote: "Children begin by loving their parents. After a time they judge them. Rarely, if ever, do they forgive them." I cannot agree with him entirely, but there is enough truth in what he says to give us pause.

3. *Revenge*. There is nothing sweet about it. As the parent-child power struggle becomes more severe, the child seeks retaliation in order to feel important. To find power he hurts others, for he is convinced that no matter what he does no one will like him.

You've seen the child who beats the dog with a hairbrush and purposely steps on his baby brother's fingers. I once spent an evening with a child who bit and scratched anyone who came within range. I had to wonder why she felt—at three years old—that life was a series of battles.

4. *Inadequacy*. When a child reaches a feeling of complete inadequacy, he gives up and refuses to become involved in anything. He sits in a corner and pouts, erecting an impenetrable wall.

By that time the parent is at his wit's end. He has no energy left with which to fight, and he too is overcome by a feeling of failure. As a result, he no longer asks the child to do anything, thus confirming the child's suspicions that he can do nothing correctly or worthwhile.

Robert L. DeBruyn, in *The Master Teacher*, says that "the change to unacceptable behavior is the most common consequence of discouragement." Children who continue to violate rules have long ago given up on trying to be good. "They are firmly convinced that acceptable behavior is beyond their grasp. With acceptable behavior they not only fail, they are a nobody. They know this is true because it has been told and proven to them time and time again by their parents as well as their teachers."[2]

What you can do

There are a number of ways to deal with misbehavior, no matter what its cause. A good first step is what T. Gordon, author of *Parent Effectiveness Training*, calls "determination," or active listening.[3] In other words, give a child time to think out a problem and come to a reasonable decision.

In a California study examining teacher-child behavior, researchers found that teachers did not give children a chance to think after a question was asked. A teacher usually will reword a question in order to help the child understand the question better. But not all children need help; they just need time to think and organize their thoughts before answering the question. Researchers recommend that teachers count to five after asking a question, in order to give children the peace and quiet needed to think.

Parents should do the same. Consider how many times you have pounced on your child, not giving him time to think or act. How often have you responded to a child's request with, "Wait a minute. I'm busy," and yet expected the child to come instantly when he is called?

A second important element of discipline is sensitivity to your own reactions. A child frequently can reduce a parent to base levels of emotional reaction. If a child knows he can "get your goat" by insisting on calling his brother a "meathead," he will do just that to provoke another explosion.

It is easy in these cases to slip into a pattern of continual verbal abuse. We lose our temper, yell irrationally, and stab our children with insults. Parents, turn down the volume; your children aren't listening.

When you are angry, try to criticize the action and not the child; correction through condemnation violates fairness. Haim Ginott, noted child psychologist and author of *Between Parent and Child*, recommends that parents stress that the action is the cause of anger and that they still care for and love the child. Don't insult your child's ego or hurt his feelings. Says Ginott, "A child needs to learn from his parents to distinguish between events that are merely unpleasant and annoying and those that are tragic or catastrophic."[4] Explain why you are angry:

"I spent all day cleaning up the house and when I see clothes all over the floor I know I have to work all over again. That makes me very angry because I am not appreciated."

Use the technique of "logical consequences." Show your child that a specific behavior will produce a specific result: If he touches the hot stove, he'll burn his hand. If he shoplifts, he'll have to face a policeman or an angry store manager.

Blind man's bluff

Some commonly used discipline techniques do not and cannot work. One is "blind man's bluff," in which parents demand blind obedience and perfect behavior by issuing empty threats. If a parent forbids a child to attend a pro football game two months from now because he stayed out too late at a party last night, the parent is probably bluffing. A week later the rage is gone, the parent feels guilty, and he is likely to back down. Score one for the child, zero for the parent. Children are experts at seeing through parental bluffs. If they know when you forbid any TV watching for a month that they will be "paroled" in a few days, your threats are weightless and your enforcement power nil.

At my institution, we teach our master's level teachers never to make threats they cannot carry out. And we teach them never to threaten a child by taking away playground time, participation in athletics, or other activities that may be the very things holding his interest in school.

Before you reach the point of making threats,

learn to recognize the situations that produce confrontations and avoid them when possible. Remove yourself from the conflict. Try to divert a young child's energies into other activities. If the child is old enough to express himself verbally, try to work out the problem together.

I believe that 90 percent of all spankings occur because we cannot verbalize our anger; therefore, in most cases, spanking is unjustifiable. Verbalizing your anger, rather than striking out in thoughtless fury, can come naturally with practice. Learn to think first and state how you feel. Examine yourself to make sure you're not overreacting and explain to the child what has made you angry. Speak up right away; don't let your displeasure simmer until it boils over. Before you spank, ask yourself if you know the reason for the child's misbehavior. What problems could be at the root of his outburst? Have you tried to talk to the child and let him speak his mind?

If you work with these techniques, you'll realize that physical punishment is not the most effective means of discipline. I believe that the parent who constantly spanks his child is a lazy disciplinarian. I have spanked my children on occasion, but for me spanking is the ultimate action, taken when these other methods fail.

I am also against corporal punishment in the schools, and I am disturbed to see it being reinstated in some school districts. The Los Angeles Board of Education recently restored limited paddling in elementary and junior high schools. Guidelines say that "one to three swats is an appropriate number for any one incident." In my opinion, one swat is too many.

What I call "counseling discipline" should be the substitute for corporal punishment. Teachers, like parents, should look for the underlying problems that produce an unruly student. School authorities should talk with parents and involve the church if possible. If these remedies prove futile, and if the child consistently disrupts class or is physically violent, he should be removed from school. Classrooms are not boxing rings, and violent students must be forced to receive their education outside the traditional school setting. They must be helped by those trained to deal with such behavior.

The "master parent"

I recommend that whenever possible teachers and parents follow some time-honored guidelines we have used with our master teachers at National College of Education. These are only a few tips for becoming a "master parent," but I believe they are ten times more constructive than using a paddle.

1. Have only a few rules. Be sure they are necessary and not just for your comfort.
2. Be consistent and impartial.
3. Enforce the rules.
4. Don't nag.
5. Use certainty of punishment, rather than severity, as a deterrent.
6. Stop the minor problems.
7. Don't be afraid to admit an error.

8. Avoid sarcasm and ridicule.
9. Be tolerant of passing fancies; give kids a chance to grow up.
10. Make yourself a model of the self-discipline you expect from children.

Finally, I do not believe the sole burden of discipline should be placed upon the father. No father wants to be greeted at the door each night by, "Johnny was bad today. You have to spank him." What kind of relationship does that create between a father and his children?

You are not alone

It should be some consolation to know that every parent has gone through, and will go through, what you are experiencing with your children. So speak up and give your misery some company.

Children need to have more adult friends than just their parents. Dr. Derek Miller says parents should ask a child one essential question: "What adult do you see frequently who is not a relative and you know accepts and loves you for what you are?"[5] If your child cannot answer that question, you should take a hard look at the opportunities you are providing for your child to know other adults.

We extend our family by spreading Thanksgiving-type dinners throughout the year. We invite other parents and their children over to dinner regularly for family fellowship. Children enjoy being around other adults, and other parents can have a positive influence when your children seem to be turning you off. Your son or daughter also can see that you are not, in fact, the meanest parent in the world. They will see that other mothers and fathers exercise discipline and insist on completed homework assignments and no candy before dinner. And you will enjoy sharing concerns with other parents.

There was a time when I thought parents "should know better." When I heard babies crying in church, I was not too far from agreeing with W. C. Fields. ("Anyone who hates children and dogs can't be all bad.") But now that I am a parent, my speeches from those days are embarrassing. The gap between my perception then and my sensitivity today is wider than I ever would have dreamed.

Gaining obedience and respect from your children and maintaining discipline can be among the most frustrating challenges of parenthood. When people come to me looking for simplistic answers, I tell them to adopt a robot. Then they can turn the switch on and off and have perfect, predictable children. We must remember that the key to spiritual growth is obedience—to God's will, God's call, and God's Word. This obedience takes strong, unceasing, daily discipline. Raising your children to be obedient and respectful is no different.

CHAPTER TEN

THE BIRDS AND THE BEES:
SEX AND YOUR CHILD

Do you remember the first time you tried to mentally picture your parents making love? The whole idea seemed ludicrous, embarrassing, or downright impossible. "Mom and Dad? Sex? You've got to be kidding!" At some point in your young life you probably attributed your existence to the stork, immaculate conception, adoption, or a miracle. Birds do it. Bees do it. But moms and dads don't do it.

For you parents who are chuckling, I've got news. Today—perhaps more so than ever before—kids do it, too. And they do it out of fear, anxiety, exaggerated expectations, and ignorance. Today our babies are having babies. More than a million teen-agers under nineteen become pregnant in America every year. Thirty thousand of them are fourteen or younger.[1] There are more than three million new cases of venereal disease in the United States each year, with the highest rate of increase in the eleven- to fifteen-year-old range. An estimated 60 percent of all young people today will have had sex before they finish high school.[2]

Our age of so-called sexual liberation is one of educational deprivation. When children confront their sexuality physically, they are unprepared emotionally and mentally because most parents, schools, and churches have done a poor job of educating them.

Viva la différence!

"Is it a boy or a girl?" That's the first question anyone asks when a child is born. And that's when parents should begin their own sex education anew. We may be shouting, "Viva la différence!" as adults, but "la différence" can be confounding when we're raising our "little men and women."

We know sex role identification develops early, but biologists and psychologists don't agree on how it happens. The biological theory says genetics and hormones are overriding factors. In fact, if a child is born with a genital abnormality (i.e., the chromosomes say "girl" and the anatomy says "boy"), it would be possible to change the child's sex without severe psychological stress only before the age of two. Later on, the change is too difficult to make. But this theory does not explain why some children behave in sexually appropriate ways and others do not.

The psychoanalytic theory says sexual identification begins between three and six, when children begin a series of experiences that lead to proper sex role development. You have probably recognized these phases in your own children.

Boys "fall in love" with their mothers (the Oedipus complex) and are hostile to their fathers. The father is seen as the powerful aggressor, but because the father has developed a relationship with the mother, a boy imitates his father's masculine traits. Freud theorized that the boy identifies with the aggressor because he is afraid his father will retaliate against his "rival" and punish him by castration.

Girls go through the same process (the Electra complex) but in a more complicated way. Although the girl's primary attachment is to her mother, she "falls in love" with her father and then becomes reattached to her mother. Freud believed girls feel that they have already been castrated.

The learning theory says parents reward and reinforce "appropriate" sex role behavior. Children are often punished for behavior parents consider inappropriate to their sex, and children learn to discriminate between "right" and "wrong."

Finally, Harvard psychologist Lawrence Kohlberg says children learn sex roles because of their intellectual organization of things in their environment. As a child becomes familiar with the term "boy" or "girl," he learns what should be included in that category. A boy may learn that footballs should be included, but dolls shouldn't. The child uses the parent of the same sex as a model.

Siblings, teachers, peers, and relatives can all influence sex role identification, but the process seems largely rooted in the home.

Can little girls be president?

From infancy on, parents do not treat boys and girls alike. Research shows baby girls are more responsive to human voices, and mothers reinforce this by verbalizing more to girls. Some say boys are more active, aggressive, willing to explore, and have better spatial sense than more verbal and passive girls. Feminists would argue this is due to social conditioning.

As a parent, you are the starring role model. You have a tremendous responsibility to give your child a right to grow up with his or her eventual career options open.* You must be careful not to stereotype children into sexually narrow roles. Once upon a time, little girls grew up to be "mommies" and housewives and, occasionally, teachers, nurses, and secretaries. Boys grew up to be "daddies," lawyers, doctors, and presidents.

It is important that children see both parents functioning in various roles. They should know that Daddy can cook dinner and do laundry and that Mommy can work and make money. Single parents should expose their children to role models of the opposite sex. Divorced mothers and fathers should be careful not to lash out against the opposite sex as "evil" in front of a child who is also that sex, or the child could become depressed about his own sexuality.

Fortunately, today we are moving away from the notion that male and female traits are at opposite poles. Researchers have concluded that masculinity

---

*(In this book I have used the pronouns "he," "his," and "him" to avoid cumbersome sentences; they in no way indicate any sexual bias.)

and femininity exist comfortably in all of us. It is entirely appropriate and possible for any one person to be dependent, assertive, and aggressive at different times. It is okay for boys and men to cry and for girls to be smart and assertive.

Even if we reinforce these ideas at home, however, we must battle the stereotypes that are beyond our control. Your child is likely to have a female teacher, while the principal and upper-level administrators are likely to be men. Although textbooks are slowly beginning to change, many still portray aggressive, achieving, dominant men and emotional, passive, subservient women. On television reruns women spend most of their time in the kitchen; rarely do they make an intelligent decision. Parents must work doubly hard to counteract these ideas when children are at an impressionable age.

The birds and the bees

Your first sexual intelligence test will come when your child asks his first question. "How did that baby get in your stomach?" "How come Daddy goes to the bathroom standing up?"

A three-year-old doesn't need to hear chapter and verse of Masters and Johnson. His questions should be answered clearly, briefly, honestly, and with proper terminology. If he asks "how the baby got in there," tell him "through sexual intercourse." He probably doesn't really want to know yet; he's just curious, and his interest will vanish as soon as his question is answered.

I can't emphasize enough how important it is to be

accurate and truthful when you answer a child's question about sex. Tell the *whole* truth at the proper time, and nothing but the truth. I remember one story about a woman who told her inquisitive young daughter that the blue box in the bathroom contained "napkins." When the mother had dinner guests one night and was frantically searching for napkins, the little girl proudly trotted out with a box of sanitary napkins. If you tell your little boy that he and Daddy have a "pee pee" and his friend at school tells him it's a "penis," he will not only be confused, but he will no longer trust your information. And if he doubts your knowledge, he will turn to other sources when he has questions.

A nationwide study done by Dr. Hershel Thornburg, professor of educational psychology at the University of Arizona in Tucson, revealed that only 8 percent of parents had discussed sex with their children. In ranking where children obtained information about sex, children put mothers fourth in importance behind schools, friends, and miscellaneous literature. Fathers contributed virtually nothing. In Dr. Thornburg's excellent book, *The Bubblegum Years*, he says only 4 percent of nine- to thirteen-year-olds discussed intercourse with their fathers; 21 percent did so with their mothers. Menstruation was discussed by 1 percent of the fathers and 8 percent of the mothers.[3]

Why? Although sex is one area in which parents cannot plead inexperience, they are decidedly short on expertise and finesse. They are too uneasy with their own sexuality to discuss the subject with their children.

THE BIRDS AND THE BEES

In a Cleveland study of how 1,400 parents handled sexual topics with their three- to eleven-year-olds, results showed predominantly "strained silence." Less than half the parents of eleven-year-olds had ever mentioned intercourse; even fewer had discussed contraception. Almost 40 percent of the girls nine to eleven years old—many of whom would soon be menstruating—had never discussed menstruation with a parent. Less than 1 percent of the mothers and less than 2 percent of the fathers had discussed wet dreams.[4]

The statistics are appalling, but not surprising. The atmosphere in many homes is not conducive to sexual communication. Parents may not openly display physical affection toward one another, and sexuality-oriented conversation is taboo at the dinner table.

Breaking this taboo is essential when your child grows older and his body matures. He'll begin to ask more and more questions, and you can give him more detailed answers.

Many parents feel they have lost control of their children from a sexual point of view. Could it be because their children have gone elsewhere to learn about it?

If you want to guide and shape your child's sexuality, you must pay the price—of whatever embarrassment it will cause you—to *talk* with him about it. Responding to a question with, "I'll tell you about it when you grow up" will only pique his curiosity and intensify his fascination with what seems forbidden and mysterious. You'll be able to judge how much information your child needs at a particular point by asking yourself why he's asking the question. If you don't know, ask him; but don't stifle him by asking accusingly, "Why do you want to know?" Answer his question *first*; then ask matter-of-factly why he is interested.

How to tell them

If you have established open lines of communication with your children, talking to them about sex should cause you no more trauma than any other subject. The best rule of thumb is to teach them a little bit at a time. Give them information gradually and naturally as questions arise.

For example, when young children ask how a baby gets out of the mother it is sufficient to tell them "through a special opening between the mother's legs." Parents can explain how the body stretches to allow the baby to grow and be born, but they should avoid frightening tales about labor pains. Children sometimes feel guilty about having caused their mother harm.

Explaining the father's role in reproduction is often the most difficult part for parents. Young children can understand that the father's body contains a special kind of seed that starts the baby growing in the mother. You can tell an older child of perhaps six or seven that the seed, called sperm, comes from the father when his penis enters the mother's vagina. Books and pamphlets can be helpful when the child is especially curious. (The National Education Association and the American Medical Association publish an excellent series of sex education pamphlets.)

THE BIRDS AND THE BEES

When children begin asking about the differences between boys and girls, be careful not to make them feel cheated. A girl should not feel she is missing out by lacking a penis, and the boy should not be dismayed when told he will never grow breasts.

Do not be shocked, shamed, or amused by your children's questions about sex. Calm and quiet explanations tell children there is nothing taboo or dirty about the subject. Unfortunately, I cannot give you a blueprint for answering all the questions that will arise. You must find the best way of explaining the story of human life to your children when they are ready.

An important fact to note here is that demonstration is *not* the way to teach children about sex. One sex counselor, believing prudery to be a great source of social problems, set up a sex education laboratory at home. He invited his son and daughter to watch him and his wife during sexual activities and permitted them to play with each other in their room.[5] A sex laboratory may teach your children what goes where, but they will learn nothing of emotions, decision-making, or relationships—the toughest sexual issues. They need to learn about love, not merely about sex.

Your pediatrician can help answer children's questions if you ask him, and the media can be an asset if you know how to use it. Although 85 percent of the TV programs from 8:00 P.M. on are for adults, plenty of kids are watching them. Parents must provide a forum where kids can discuss the things they see on TV that they don't understand. Children need an adult to interpret issues like abortion and prostitution. When children read advertisements for movies like *The American Gigolo*, how many of them know what a gigolo is? You can also sit down with your children and read—together—books expressly written to help children understand sex.

One thing is certain: Your child will learn about sex. Our generation did, and all too often it was on the street or in the back seat of a car. You cannot protect your child from information by ignoring the whole subject. If you leave your child in a sexual void, he will fill it with information—right or wrong—from any source he can find.

Misconceptions about conception

One pregnant girl thought she couldn't become pregnant if she had intercourse standing up. Another was certain that sex during her menstrual cycle was safe. One adolescent father had assured his girlfriend they were "safe" because he had not been circumcised. A dismayed teen-aged mother-to-be thought she had taken adequate precautions—she had swallowed an entire can of contraceptive foam.[6]

Aaron Hass, U.C.L.A. sex therapist and author of *Teenage Sexuality*, says most teens get their information from such magazines as *Playboy, Playgirl,* and *Penthouse.*[7] Hass surveyed 625 teens nationwide between the ages of fifteen and eighteen. "Pornography fills the void created by the lack of

146

education provided by parents and teachers," Hass reports. "It is the source of information for most teen-agers who have no one to talk to about sex."

Hass's research also shattered a common parental belief. Far from being preoccupied with sex, teenagers ranked it as relatively unimportant, far down the list from doing well in school (ranked first) and making friends. They see sex as a means of communicating love and affection, "not simply as a physical release."[8]

They nevertheless enter the sexual realm in ignorance. Less than 30 percent of sexually active teenagers use any form of birth control. According to the Alan Guttmacher Institute, a research arm of Planned Parenthood, only 300,000 of the million teen-age girls who become pregnant each year are married when their babies are born; 100,000 marry after giving birth; 300,000 have abortions, and 200,000 miscarry.[9] A girl can suffer any one of those experiences without having the slightest idea about how she became pregnant, and her boyfriend may be no more enlightened.

Who should teach these children? We parents must.

Sex in the halls, but not in the classroom

In the United States there are no laws that say courses in sex education must be taught in all public schools. A few countries are more "progressive." In Denmark, Sweden, Czechoslovakia, and East Germany, sex education is compulsory. West Germany is the only non-Scandinavian or non-East European country where sex education is found in the daily school curriculum.[10] We Americans join the majority of countries in their reluctance to formally teach children about a perfectly natural fact of life.

In a number of states it is not uncommon for any discussion of birth control, masturbation, or abortion to be illegal in the classroom. (In those states, teen-age pregnancy rates are highest. They are lowest in New York City, where high schools have birth-control clinics.)

We have come to equate sexual knowledge with promiscuity: "If they learn about it, they'll do it!" Look, they will learn about it *anyway*. Isn't it better for children to learn about sex in school rather than on the streets? I feel sex education should be a vital part of our schools—as well as our homes and churches. Starting with fish tanks and rabbits in kindergarten through to teaching marital reproduction, pregnancy, birth control, divorce, and homosexuality in high school.

We have spoken throughout this book about children's rights. Do they not have a right to know about their own bodies? Do they not have a right to be informed sexual beings?

In our free sexual environment today, it is more and more difficult for teen-agers to resist sexual temptation. They face tremendous peer pressure. I say virgins have rights too! To give a child the courage of his convictions, we parents must lay a solid foundation of knowledge and values.

THE BIRDS AND THE BEES
From the heart

There is no foolproof formula for teaching children to become sexually responsible adults. But in addition to the suggestions mentioned throughout this chapter, I would give you, as a parent, this advice.

1. Develop in your children a feeling of positive self-worth. People who feel good about themselves are not the ones getting V.D. at thirteen.
2. Love your children excessively. We constantly hear teen-age girls say they want to have babies so they will have "someone to love them." You are the someone who must love your children.
3. Teach respect for your body. If children see you abusing your body by overeating and getting little exercise as you grow older, what does that teach them? It tells them they should give in to every bodily desire and whim without restraint.
4. Reinforce high moral behavior. Discuss values with your children. If a boy is pressuring your daughter for sex, ask her what she really wants out of that relationship. Tell her she has a right not to be exploited. Tell her you are proud of her for refusing to do something "because everyone else does it." Parents continually major in the minor issues, such as how long a boy's hair is or how short a girl's skirt is. Express your views on sideburns and hemlines, but concentrate on your children's inner selves.
5. Continue to be open and honest. If you have

made mistakes in the past, admit them candidly. Your children will probably understand.

Finally, teach your children about love. The complete union of two human beings is the most beautiful experience known to man. We seem to concentrate on teaching children sexual mechanics, while we neglect to delve deeply into the heart. If *you* teach *them* from your heart, they will tend to act more wisely with their bodies.

CHAPTER ELEVEN

THE TWENTY-ONE COMMANDMENTS OF GOOD OLD-FASHIONED PARENTING

Through the years I have learned a great deal about childrearing, mostly by the trial-and-error method. I still do not know everything about parenting, but I would like to share with you twenty-one "commandments" that have helped and guided me in the effort to be a good parent.

1. Love unconditionally.

As God's love is unconditional to us, so our love for our children should be unconditional. I recall the illustration of a father who always told his children that no matter what they did, no matter what kind of trouble they were in, they could call him and he would bring them home without interrogation. He received only one phone call when his children were growing up—once when his daughter found herself in a situation where she didn't belong. She knew her father would love her no less for admitting that mistake.

I know parents who hand out hugs as prizes and who teach their kids to bargain with love as if it were just another commodity. I know parents who threaten to "disown" their teen-age daughters if they ever become pregnant, and who have banished children from their homes for adopting beliefs contrary to their own. The good child receives love as his reward; the bad child receives none as his punishment.

I am by no means saying that unconditional love means doing away with discipline and giving children a license to behave in any manner they choose. I am saying that we may take away the television program or the chocolate cake in the best interests of our children, but we must never place stipulations on our love. Our loving arms must always be open to our children.

2. Do unto your mate as you would have your children do unto others.

The way you treat your mate shows your children how other human beings should be treated. You and your spouse provide the most detailed model of a relationship, and children will be quick to mimic your behavior—good or bad.

Children notice if you treat your mate differently in public than you do in private. They will notice if you are a marital chameleon who feigns affection at parties and perpetually finds fault at home. Children learn early the lessons of hypocrisy and insincerity. Some couples make no attempt at a "cover-up."

I know one bright, attractive couple who constantly compete with each other. In public, they practice a never-ending game of one-upmanship. It would seem that this couple is giving their children everything, and materially they may be. But I can guess how those children treat their friends and how they will treat their future spouses.

Children will see you when you're impatient and irritable and will see how you vent your frustrations on your mate. But they will also see how you apologize, how you handle forgiveness. If you want to teach your children to treat others with kindness, concern, and fairness, you and your mate must set that example.

3. Deal with yourself.

Much of what you do as a parent is a product of past conditioning. You're following the patterns of your parents or your friends who are parents. Your actions are a natural result of the attitudes ingrained in you.

We all have bad habits and shortcomings. But it is critical that we try to understand them and deal with them if we are to do our best job as parents. The behavior you hate in your child may be your own. His insecurities may be your insecurities. Don't lash out against your child instead of holding a mirror to your own personality and trying to correct what you dislike in yourself.

Recognize actions that activate your temper. Analyze what types of behavior from others elicit unreasonable responses from you. A bad case of overreaction may reflect a long-buried trauma from your own childhood.

When I was in high school I was co-captain of the football team and a member of the church choir. The only night the choir rehearsed was Thursday night, the night when the football team went to a movie together. I remember receiving a great deal of parental approval for choosing to go to choir rehearsal. But I'm not sure I'd make the same choice again.

If my own child were faced with the same dilemma, would I encourage him to skip choir practice in order for him to recapture what I feel I missed? Would I be able to step away from what would be an emotional situation for me and allow my child to make his own choice? These are the kinds of questions you must answer deep within yourself if you are to grow as a parent and a person.

4. Take time to be with your children.

In my youth we had a motto: "Three things come not back: time passed, spoken word, and neglected opportunity." I think that applies to parenting. The time when your daughter starred in the school play or your son hit a home run will not come back. You must be there to capture the moment. *Parenting takes time.* There are no shortcuts. If you make the commitment to be a parent, you must be willing to sacrifice your Saturday golf game for your child's Saturday football game.

We hear much talk about spending "quality time" with our children. I believe all time spent with children should be quality time, and I'm not talking about occasional trips to Disneyland. Your child neither wants those trips nor expects them often.

Your child will value a ten-minute game of catch more than five rides on the roller coaster when you haven't said hello to him in a month. "I'll make it up to you" is an empty promise. You can't make up for missed birthdays and missed graduations.

Someone else can chair the committee, someone else can sing in the choir, someone else can serve on the board. But I don't want anyone else to be my children's father.

5. *Create a proper environment in the home.*

It is up to you to create the kind of "society" you want in your home, whether it be democratic or autocratic. You create the atmosphere and the mood in the "little world" that is your home. You have the power to create a warm and loving retreat where all family members have a voice and where they share in each other's pleasure and pain.

Even good parents can unwittingly become dictators because that is—or seems to be—the easiest style of leadership. Family teamwork takes more work, cooperation, and understanding. My wife, Donna, has done a much better job than I have at never shutting the door on our children. I have never heard her say, "We can't do that." She doesn't build unnecessary expectations, yet she remains open to the possibilities. A good example of our family style is the matter of family vacations—always a joint decision. Vacations are a small part of family life, perhaps, but they may be the most exciting times of the year for a child. When you ask him his opinion, you're telling him that he matters.

In addition to creating teamwork in my home, I've also tried to leave the disappointments and frustrations of the day outside the door. I try to maintain an upbeat atmosphere where my children can become recharged with optimism and enthusiasm for the next day. I know that if I've had a bad day I can cast a dark shadow over an entire evening—and it may be the same evening my son will be bursting with pride over a test score. For each member of my family, I want "coming home" to be a pleasure.

6. Clearly communicate freedoms and limitations.

Don't assume your children know where their boundaries lie. Tell them—directly and clearly. Children need and want boundaries. I tell my children what places they can go, what they can do, and how they should act. I tell them when I want them home on week nights and weekends. I make it clear I expect them to attend church with us on Sunday, no matter how late they stay up on Saturday night. I tell them I expect them to take care of themselves physically, and if I see them taking on too many activities, I apply the brakes.

Both children and parents are more at ease with clearly stated guidelines. My children have not tried to stretch their freedoms, and I have loosened their ties as they have demonstrated increased responsibility and maturity. I have not adhered to strict age guidelines; each of my children has been ready for certain responsibilities at a different age.

In a society grappling with permissiveness, it is

156

crucial that parents give children a "map" to follow throughout their growth.

7. *Be your own family.*

Keeping up with the Joneses can be ruinous. Your children are nothing like your neighbors' kids. Mr. and Mrs. Jones are unlike you and your spouse. So what makes you think they're the experts on raising *your* children? When Johnny pleads to have a car "because everyone else does," do you succumb for his own sake or for yours?

You need not reject everything another family does; you can certainly learn from shared experiences. But your own common sense—and a higher form of guidance than the Joneses—are your best teachers.

I have never tried to model my family after someone else's. I have found that children's interests go as quickly as they come. This week Mark wants a Z-28; next week he'll want a Mercedes. This year the rage is racquetball; next year it will be soccer. I have no intention of going into debt because every teenaged kid on the block has a car. By the same token, maybe my child *does* need a car when no other family can afford one.

8. *Be consistent, yet flexible.*

When you're dealing with human behavior, no man-made rules are absolute. I am firm when I believe a rule is correct and just, but I am not so rigid that I cannot bend when I learn new information. As an educator, I realize I must respond to new

knowledge. If I permitted my children to drink alcohol, thinking it had no harmful side effects what-
soever, and suddenly learned that the exact opposite
was the case, I would change my rule. If I forbade my
children to associate with certain friends and later
discovered I was mistaken, I would amend my rule.
A parent who holds to rules just to demonstrate his
authority is telling a child the rule itself is more
important than the reason behind it or the people
who are affected.

I see parents every week who rigidly use the
brick-and-mortar principle of rule-making in their
homes. They build restrictions that they refuse to
knock down for any reason. To them issues are black
and white, never grey. I am convinced that overly
rigid parents will produce children who are just as
troubled as those from permissive parents. Be tough,
yes; but be fair.

9. *Identify with your children.*

Perhaps I am reinforcing a stereotype, but I believe wives often do a much better job of identifying
with children than husbands do. My wife is the one
who stops me when I rush to turn off the rock music
station on the car radio. "Have you really listened to
that music?" she'll ask me. Frankly, I haven't; I
happen to love soft music. But I am sometimes too
quick to condemn what is important to my children.

I always have to remind myself that I was once a
child, but my kids have never been adults. I am the
one who must say to my children, "I understand
what you're going through; I understand where you

are." Parents must stretch and bend a bit, even if it's a long reach back to adolescence. You needn't be "one of the kids" again, but you can be patient with their fads and follies.

10. Participate in projects with your children.

Help your child with his homework or his school project, or join in on his hobby. These kinds of activities provide an opportunity for closeness that may surprise you. When you take interest in Tommy's science project, you're taking an interest in Tommy. You're teaching him to be creative, and you're showing him how to resolve dilemmas.

One of the most crushing blows you can give a child is to take no interest in an accomplishment or project close to his heart. One child I know of ran home one afternoon with the exciting news that she had just won first place in the spelling bee. Her mother, preoccupied with herself and an unusually frustrating day, scarcely acknowledged the child's presence, much less her achievement. On the other side of the coin, I can remember the many speeches I had to give because I held leadership positions in school. My mother was always by my side to help me. You will regret it if you don't create that kind of memory for your own child.

11. Be willing to take a stand.

Weak children are the products of weak parents. Children need to look up to a pillar of strength in the family, and although they may not always admit it to you, they are proud when you demonstrate conviction.

When I see friends of my children trying to use them or take advantage of them, I take a stand. When I see parents in the church or community backing away from issues, I come forth. I am beginning to see the same quality emerging in my children, and I am proud. My sons, Morgan and Mark, are leaders in their school. They take stands against alcohol, drugs, and smoking, although many seek to influence them the other way. They stand strong, and their friends respect them for it. That tells me I am doing my job.

12. Turn negatives into positives.

This may be the most frequently violated parental commandment. Just the other day I overheard a parent say to a child, "You'll never learn. You'll never learn." After two months of that negative suggestion, the child probably won't learn. "That's a stupid thing to do." "I knew you'd get your new dress filthy." "You never come home on time." Do any of these sound familiar?

It takes very little to destroy a child's self-confidence. But that's what we're doing when we dwell on his weaknesses and overlook his strengths. Why not start believing the glass is half full instead of half empty? Try telling your child, "I'm glad to see you went to bed early tonight," instead of, "It's about time you got some rest."

Think of how you would react if your boss treated you the same way you often treat your children.

13. *Open your home to others.*

Invite other families and friends into your home to show your children that friendship is important. Whenever possible, I include my friends' children in dinner or party invitations. I don't want to be responsible for depriving them of an opportunity for family togetherness, and all of us can enjoy the visit more.

I also encourage my children to bring their own friends into our home, and they have never hesitated to do so. If I close my home to these young people, they might find another, less desirable place to spend the evening. Like any parent, I like to know where my children are. I am willing to suffer the slight inconvenience of noise and music for my own peace of mind.

14. *Maintain realistic expectations.*

No one is perfect; don't expect it of yourself or of your children. Don't force your own unrealized expectations upon your child. You may want him to write the Great American Novel, but he may be struggling through remedial English. Don't expect him to mature instantly, to always make correct judgments. Don't rush him through his childhood.

I know how tempting it is to try to live vicariously through your children, when you've spent so many years hoping and planning even before they were born. It's human nature to want your child to go to college if you missed the chance; but if he has the talent and desire to be an auto mechanic, it is unfair to interfere. We must give our children the freedom to use their own yardsticks for peace and success.

15. Show respect for your own parents.

If you expect your children to treat you with respect and consideration, be careful about how you behave toward your own parents. Are you constantly complaining about Grandma? Do you dread her visits and bemoan your obligation? Stop and think what will happen when you become Grandma or Grandpa.

While it is true that older people often become absentminded and ill, perhaps it is because we strip them of their dignity and usefulness. In our Western culture, we do not accord senior citizens the rights and regard they deserve.

I will, however, add a word to grandparents: try not to pressure your children and become possessive about your grandchildren. Remember that your children may not be able to spend as much time with you as they would like because they have their own families now. You were once in their place; let your understanding span the generation gap.

16. Plan family activities.

The family that plays—and prays—together, stays together. Nothing can take the place of a family activity, no matter how simple. Every Sunday my family goes out to lunch after church. It's been one of our most treasured traditions, and I make every effort to see it gets high priority. A family activity can be a walk down the street in the evening, or a trip to the store. It can be a game of Scrabble or Monopoly.

I have made popcorn with my kids, colored Easter eggs, and put puzzles together. I have played checkers and football, gone to museums and amusement parks. The activity itself is relatively unimportant; what renews our spirits is the feeling of togetherness, the bonds that become stronger each time we all embark on a new adventure.

17. *Keep your sense of humor.*

Don't take parenting too seriously. I know full well how exhausting parenting is, how it tests your mettle to the nth degree, how important it is to be a good parent. But that doesn't mean you should wait eighteen years before cracking a smile. Kids can be hilarious. *You* can be hilarious sometimes when you try to be an ogre and you find you're way off base. Laugh at yourself. Laugh with your kids. Laughter can drown a multitude of sorrows and tensions before they turn into tears.

The world has enough gloomy, frowning faces; bring home a smile and share it with your kids.

18. *Explain your actions.*

Tell your children why you became angry in a certain situation. Anger most often originates outside the home, and your reaction to a child's minor infraction can puzzle and frighten him. You're human; you'll blow your top occasionally. But when you cool off, explain yourself. "I really got angry at you unnecessarily because I had a bad day at work."

When you create rules, be sure to explain them. "Because I said so" or "because I'm your father" is not sufficient. Your child may not like the rule even after you explain it, but he'll understand that you're not being arbitrary. When a friend of mine was young, her father refused to allow her on a motorcycle because he believed they were unsafe. She protested the rule continually, because her boyfriend rode a motorcycle. The rule remained, the boyfriend moved on, and the daughter still respected her father for thinking first of her safety.

19. Establish trust as a norm.

Trust is the bottom line of parenting. My wife and I both came from homes based on trust, between husband and wife as well as between parent and child. Your children will honor the trust you place in them. We have always told our children that we trust them to make the right decision in any situation, because we know we have instilled deep moral and spiritual values in them.

If you find yourself constantly questioning your mate or your children, you should ask yourself why. Ask if they've given you reason to doubt them or if it's yourself you mistrust. Do you trust your own fidelity as a mate? Do you trust your own judgment as a parent? If you want and expect trust, it will be the norm in your home.

20. Work.

You have to work at good parenting. It's a full-time job that most of us must do part time. Being a good parent means learning everything we can about this all-important task—becoming educated, informed, responsible. Work means tackling problems head-on when they arise and seeking help when you need it.

I know some very hard-working adults who are very lazy parents. They don't bring the same kind of dedication to their childrearing that they bring to their sixty-hour-a-week jobs. These otherwise intelligent people somehow believe their children are going to rear themselves.

21. Enjoy your children.

Sit back and relax. For every husband, I wish a wife who loves children. For every wife, I wish a husband who does the same. Enjoyment is part of the blessing of children, the blessing of including them in your life. Rediscover the world through the eyes of your children. Don't miss out. They will never be this age again.

CHAPTER TWELVE

FUTURE CHILD: A SHOCKING LOOK

Any time we deal with the future, we're groping in the dark. Our crystal balls are cloudy, at best. But when it comes to tomorrow's child, I can make one prediction without reservation: Deep-down inside, he will not differ from today's child. He will still need love and affection every year of his life. He will seek friendship, acceptance, and assurance from family and friends. The future child will need his parents to help mold his personality and to help resolve his confusion about the physical as well as the spiritual world.

The child will not change in the years ahead. But tomorrow's husband and wife will deliver that child—bravely or not—into an entirely new world. Our environment will be altered in some ways that we already expect and in other ways that will surprise and even shock us.

A number of changes appear likely at this point:

- Our society will be far less child-centered.
- The family unit will come under increasing pressure.

- Technology—and the media in particular—will fight us for control of our children.
- Sexual roles will be redefined.
- Education and business will mesh.
- Rising inflation and the threat of war will restrict our lifestyles.

A world for the small?

Once upon a time, it was fun to be a kid. It was even *okay* to be a kid. Today, and in all likelihood tomorrow, we hurl our children headlong into adulthood. As one sixteen-year-old put it:

> If you don't act old, you get lost, the world passes by without you. ... You rush yourself to grow up. You push, they push, and then when you get there— wherever *there* is—you realize you've come up out of the ground into, like an empty cave. There's nothing in it at all. It's just a cold, empty cave. Right now, that's the way the future looks to me. ... You hate to admit it, but there are lots of times you wish you still *were* a little kid nodding at all the questions people ask.[1]

As our society places greater emphasis on the aged, we are entering a world "far less child-centered than our own," says futurist Alvin Toffler in his new book, *The Third Wave*. Toffler describes the "Second Wave" era.

> Millions of American parents lived out their own dreams through their children—often because they could reasonably expect their children to do better socially and economically than they, themselves, had

167

done. This expectation of upward mobility encouraged parents to concentrate enormous psychic energies on their children. Today, many middle-class parents face agonizing disillusionment as their children—in a far more difficult world—move down, rather than up, the socioeconomic scale. The likelihood of surrogate fulfillment is evaporating.

For all these reasons, the baby born tomorrow may well enter a society no longer obsessed with—perhaps not even terribly interested in—the needs, wants, psychological development, and instant gratification of the child.[2]

Childhood will be more demanding and structured, says Toffler. Parents will be less permissive, and childhood will shrink. The forces tugging at our children will be stronger, but Toffler suggests that more responsible and productive youth "may well turn out to be the high achievers of tomorrow."

All in the family?

The family unit as we know it may be the oddity of the future. Test-tube babies and sperm banks will cast a new light on tomorrow's decision to become parents, and we will see radical experiments with childbearing and childrearing. More and more, your children's playmates will come from single-parent homes or two-paycheck homes. We know that the traditional family with working father and stay-at-home mother is becoming a myth; it is predicted that by 1990, 60 percent of all adult women will be in the labor force. Over half of our children under the age of eighteen have working mothers. The children come home from school to empty houses and television sets. Part-time parents deposit children too small for elementary grades at tennis clubs or nursery schools. We see picture-window children wearing monogrammed sweaters and tiny fur coats, when they need to be swathed in attention and affection.

One out of three marriages currently ends in divorce, and predictions say the number may rise to half of all marriages.[3] For children of divorce, parental harmony will be mere fiction. Mothers and fathers will play musical custody as children try to decide whom to love best.

Julius Segal and Herbert Yahraes, in their book *A Child's Journey: Forces That Shape the Lives of Our Young,* give this warning.

> The stresses endured by adults cannot be hidden from the child's view altogether—nor should they. But neither ought children become the chronic targets for parental conflicts and passions. . . . In resolving their discord, parents owe it to their children to protect them from becoming innocent casualties of the emotional warfare waged daily in so many homes.[4]

That the family structure would change was inevitable. But if the family is to survive at all—and it must for the good of the children—we must see:

- a resurgence of love for children and for each other.
- a return to sacrifice for the sake of the chil-

dren, instead of sacrificing the children for
our own sake.

- a look-before-you-leap philosophy of parenting: careful consideration before conception
and parent training courses that take the be-
wilderment out of childrearing.
- the preservation of human interaction in an
advanced technological society. Mechaniza-
tion should complement, rather than
supplant and undermine, the relationship between parent and child.
- increased government and corporate support
for superior day care, including flexible working hours for mothers and fathers.
- public recognition and support for both the
mothering and fathering role in society.

I urge you to plan a new strategy for family survival. Return to the ways of the past to find joy in the
future. Plan inexpensive family weekends and vacations close to home. Look to each other for strength
and solace.

Have the courage to refuse time-demanding job
promotions. I applaud business leaders who work to
ease the burden on their employees and who do not
penalize the person who confines work to the hours
between nine and five. Outside forces are all too
eager to fill the gap left by absent mothers and
fathers. In order to take charge of your children's
lives, you parents must be in control. Says Kenneth
Keniston and the Carnegie Council on Children:

FUTURE CHILD: A SHOCKING LOOK

To be effective coordinators of the people and forces that are shaping their children, parents must have a voice in how they proceed, and a wide choice so they do not have to rely on people or programs they do not respect. Parents who are secure, supported, valued, and in control of their lives are more effective parents than those who feel unsure and who are not in control.[5]

Technological warfare

The future will attack us with technology and media whose messages we may not want our children to heed. We will have to fight hard to see that our children's minds and imaginations are not violated.

I hope you will give your own children some "elbow room" in the future, some quiet time and space to breathe and ponder. I often think this is the chief reason why we haven't seen any Einsteins or da Vincis lately. Life is too loud. With stimuli bombarding us from every angle, how can we reach into the mind's darkest recesses and unlock its secrets? Most of us have our creative thoughts in the shower, in the bathroom, while we're brushing our teeth, and as we drift off to sleep. It is at those times that our thoughts can wander—if we let them—and new ideas can swim through the muck of worries and plans. Children need the same experience, and we must make space in their lives for creativity.

The coming decades will be instantaneous, not spontaneous; they will be video-, audio-, and battery-powered. Our children will have access to toys, games, electronic wizardry, sophisticated gadgets, and gizmos they may understand better than we do. Perhaps we will need to wage "the moral equivalent of war" against television. When we do use TV, we should tune in cable channels and educational programs and tune out the thousands of commercials and the "sit-com" drivel. Your child does not need entertainment served on a silver platter.

Your child's own instincts and your guidance are the best prescription for original thought. Don't buy every flashy "thing" on the market. Keep your child's life simple. Help him discover books and the out-of-doors. Introduce your child to another age when the tide rolling in and the setting sun were the wonders of the world. Infants born today, and infants who will be born tomorrow, have the same creativity the babies of yesterday possessed; but we stifle it unknowingly before it has a chance to develop. Let your child explore his inner and outer world without being plugged in and artificially turned on.

Turn off technology and turn on human relationships. Your child will not learn how to resolve conflicts by watching TV or by playing electronic ping-pong. He will learn it when he plays with his friends and when you teach him how to handle disagreements. Preserve for your child the "humanness" of life apart from knobs, switches, and buttons.

Sexuality: a new style

Children of the future will still ask the same kinds of probing questions they ask today when they try to sort out their "maleness" and "femaleness." This may be one area where, as a parent, you may think you can be smugly confident. After all, boys will still be boys and girls will be girls, no matter how modern we are.

It isn't that simple. We will no longer be able to rely on stereotypes to provide male and female role models—and well we shouldn't. The eighties and nineties will demand that we search for new definitions of masculinity and femininity—for our own benefit as well as for that of our children. The distinctions will be blurred in young eyes, and we will have to work harder to show boys and girls the way to their own sexual identity.

To be fully masculine will mean you have access to the range of expression traditionally open only to women. To be fully feminine will mean you have access to opportunities traditionally open only to men. Men will be tough, yet tender—providers as well as cooks and housekeepers. Women will be strong, yet sensitive—achievers who still remember to applaud the achievements of others.

Children still need to see a difference between men and women, however, and we must come to grips with how we want to teach them that lesson. Adequate role models will be essential. As Segal and Yahraes remind us:

In families shorn of the father's positive influence, adult male surrogates are needed to enrich the child's emotional resources. Warm and supportive masculine figures—whether stepfathers, members of the

173

extended family, leaders of social organizations, **or** teachers—can substitute as male models and become beacons of security in the often uncertain world of the growing child.[6]

Sex education in the school, church, and home will be critical in the coming years. Ignorance of the "facts of life," disrespect for the human body, and disregard for morality have created a generation of sexually permissive youngsters. If we do not lift our heads from the sand and begin educating our children about sex at an early age, history will be doomed to repetition. Parents, learn to deal with your own sexuality through counseling and education, so you can respond intelligently when children need answers.

The public school bell tolls

The complexion of education will change dramatically in the future. Children will begin school earlier, perhaps as young as two, and complete high school by age fourteen. As much learning will occur outside the classroom as inside, and the academic world will mesh with the working world throughout a person's life. We will see a new spirit of acceptance and dignity for the trades. In a world strapped for energy and food, children will learn again the art of survival.

We will see improved teaching and smaller classes as public school enrollments decline. We will see old buildings remodeled and used as schools by day and as recreation centers by night. We will see the advent of the teacher's doctorate—a new type of degree, practically devised and geared for the classroom instructor. (As one dean of a prestigious university told me, "If they call people who treat our dogs doctors, shouldn't they call the people who teach our children doctors as well?")

We will see creative and special programs slashed from tight budgets, and the gifted and the handicapped will suffer because of it. Public schools will become poverty-ridden, and the private and public sector will compete for funds. Public schools will be squeezed financially—on the local level by citizens who oppose property tax increases, and on the federal level by competition for tax dollars from other interests. We may see the neighborhood school vanish forever, and continue to hear parents demand that schools be held accountable for students who fail to learn.

As an educator, I fervently wish I could be more optimistic. I urge parents and communities to marshal support for the public schools lest quality education become the domain of the affluent. Spend your money on solid educational programs and salaries for high-caliber teachers. Make learning a twenty-four-hour-a-day process in your home; teach the pleasures of knowledge and be a model "learner" yourself.

A world at war?

Much as I hate to say it, I believe the future child will live under the looming possibility of war. We can't ignore the headlines that speak of strife in every corner of the world. The child of tomorrow will have to plan his education and his career with military service in the back of his mind. The parents of the future may see their children die for their country. More women may have to raise children alone.

At the same time, the strain of economic pressures will tighten belts to the last notch. Cars will no longer be teen-agers' toys, and extravagant vacations will be a memory. Perhaps children will learn to value a dollar again and will develop an old-fashioned regard for earning money.

How will we cope with these possibilities? Is there any hope for the future?

Absolutely! With each child that comes into this world there is new hope and a new chance to restore faith. I am talking not only about faith in God, but proper confidence in ourselves and in each other. Our children will not turn to drugs, alcohol, and religious cults if we parents help them discover a greater reason for living. They will not find it in money or power, in things or on television. They will find it when we parents give them a moral and spiritual backbone that keeps them standing erect and proud.

ACKNOWLEDGMENTS

This book required a considerable amount of research; each chapter could have been expanded to a book. I am grateful for the many people who contributed solid research, my many gifted administrators and faculty members who were willing to share their extraordinary expertise and insight.

I thank Dr. Lynn McCarthy, director of National College's private elementary and middle school, the Baker Demonstration School, for assisting with the research on creativity and obedience; Dr. Mary Alice Freeman, director of Special Education Programs, who helped us remember the very special children; Joan Smutny, director of Job Creation Program and director of Gifted Programs, for sharing her knowledge about an often-neglected group; Dr. Rita Weinberg, practicing psychologist and chair of the Psychology Department, for her thorough research on the stages of growth, sexuality, and education; and her husband, Dr. S. Kirson Weinberg, whose major study on incest was invaluable; Dr. Jack Sturch, my assistant, for his untiring help throughout the

177

writing of the book; Bob Myers, director of Professional Publications and Educational Resources in the School of Continuing Studies, for his research and guidance; Marilyn Lester and Gertrude Weinstein of National College's library, for checking every source in their extensive search for material; Dr. Darrell Bloom, dean of National's Graduate School, a true "master teacher," for his book and suggestions; Dr. Sherrel Bergmann, associate dean of National's Graduate School, for "teaching" me about sex education; Dr. Sidney Tickton, formerly of the Ford Foundation and now vice president of the Academy of Educational Development in New York and Washington, D. C., who helped me brainstorm ideas until they became more clearly defined; Dr. Glenn Heck, vice president for Academic Affairs at National College, who has been a constant source of strength; Betty Weeks, director of Early Childhood Program, the Foster G. McGaw Graduate School, and the senior kindergarten in the Baker Demonstration School, Wanda Lincoln, Master Teacher in Residence at the Kohl Teacher Center and teacher at the Library/Media Center of the Baker Demonstration School, and Betty Jane Wagner, chair of the Humanities Division, for their contributions on child development and creativity; Robin Wright and her food service staff, for providing sustenance during the long office nights of work; and Betsy Edwards, my secretary, who typed the manuscript with love and care.

I would like to thank Peter Gillquist of Thomas Nelson for his keen editorial sense, and Larry Stone,

ACKNOWLEDGMENTS

also of Thomas Nelson, for his much-needed encouragement.

As I examined the research on children's rights, I had to make many tough decisions about what to include in this book. Laura Allen Engleman was my right hand in helping me clarify what I really wanted to say. Her unusual editorial skills were tested time and time again as we revised each chapter, and the depth of her creativity and the loving care with which she helped weave the words are evident on every page.

Those of you who are married know that a mate is an integral part of any project of this magnitude. This is the sixth book I've been involved with, and I am so thankful for my wife, Donna, who encourages me, who understands a mind preoccupied with organization and eyes that tire from research, who realizes that a manuscript does not develop overnight, and who knows I need her love and support.

NOTES

Chapter 1

1. Beatrice and Ronald Gross, *The Children's Rights Movement* (Garden City, N.Y.: Anchor Books, 1977), p. 350.
2. "Children of the World: Rights & Realities," *Social Education,* vol. 43, no. 1 (January, 1979), pp. 41–42.
3. 1978 Annual Report of the Children's Defense Fund, 1520 New Hampshire Ave., N.W., Washington, D. C. 20036, pp. 2–6.
4. Pat Wald, "Making Sense Out of the Rights of Youth," *Child Welfare,* vol. 55, no. 6 (June, 1976), pp. 379-80.
5. Ernest Hollings, *The Case Against Hunger* (n.p., 1970).
6. Gross and Gross, *Children's Rights,* p. 16.
7. Ibid., pp. 87–89.
8. Carl F. Calkins, Ronald W. Lukenbill, and William J. Mateer, "Children's Rights: An Introductory Sociological Overview," *Peabody Journal of Education,* vol. 50, no. 2 (January, 1973), pp. 89–90.
9. 1978 Annual Report of the Children's Defense Fund, p. 10.
10. "Child Abuse and Neglect in the American Society," *The Center Magazine,* vol. 11, no. 2 (April/May, 1978), p. 72.
11. John Holt, *Escape from Childhood: The Needs and Rights of Children* (New York: E. P. Dutton, 1974), pp. 18–19.

Chapter 2

1. "Prevent Child Abuse," National Committee for Prevention of Child Abuse, 111 E. Wacker Drive, Suite 510, Chicago, Ill. 60601.

NOTES

2. "Child Abuse and Neglect in the American Society," *The Center Magazine,* vol. 11, no. 2 (May/April, 1978), pp. 70–77.
3. Ibid., p. 71.
4. Ibid., p. 73.
5. Roland Summit and Jo Ann Kryso, "Sexual Abuse of Children: A Clinical Spectrum," *American Journal of Orthopsychiatry,* vol. 48, no. 2 (April, 1978), p. 246.
6. "Prevent Child Abuse."
7. Charles E. Gentry, "Incestuous Abuse of Children: The Need for an Objective View," *Child Welfare,* vol. 57, no. 6 (June, 1978), p. 362.
8. Verna Jones, "Incest: When Misguided Affection Pulls Family Members Astray," *Suburban Trib* of Chicago *Tribune,* March 17, 1980.
9. Summit and Kryso, "Sexual Abuse," p. 245.
10. Ibid.
11. "Attacking the Last Taboo," *Time,* April 14, 1980, p. 72.
12. Laura Green, "Abusive Parents," Chicago *Sun-Times,* March 6, 1980.
13. "Child Abuse and Neglect," p. 71.
14. Ibid., p. 72.
15. Albert Rosenfield, "The 'Elastic Mind' Movement: Rationalizing Child Neglect?" *Saturday Review,* April 1, 1978, pp. 26–28.
16. Ibid., p. 27.
17. Ibid.
18. Perry Duryea, Vincent J. Fontana, and Jose D. Alfaro, "Child Maltreatment: A New Approach In Educational Programs," *Children Today,* vol. 7, no. 5 (September/October, 1978), pp. 13–16.
19. James S. Dobson, *The Strong-Willed Child* (Wheaton, Ill.: Tyndale House, 1978), p. 141.
20. Rogers Worthington, "Will Durant: Still exploring times of man," Chicago *Tribune,* March 24, 1980.

Chapter 3

1. Beatrice and Ronald Gross, *The Children's Rights Movement* (Garden City, N.Y.: Anchor Books, 1977), pp. 48–55.
2. Albert E. Wilkerson, *The Rights of Children: Emergent Concepts in Law and Society* (Philadelphia: Temple University Press, 1973), p. 253.

3. Michael S. Wald, editorial, *Child Development,* vol. 47, no. 1 (March, 1976), pp. 1–5.
4. Ibid., p. 4.
5. "The Children of Divorce," *Newsweek,* Feb. 11, 1980.
6. Shirley Soman, *Let's Stop Destroying Our Children* (New York: Hawthorn Books, 1974), pp. 3–8.
7. Ibid., pp. 20ff.
8. Pat Wald, "Making Sense Out of the Rights of Youth," *Child Welfare,* vol. 55, no. 6 (June, 1976), p. 386.
9. Kenneth Keniston, *All Our Children: The American Family Under Pressure* (New York and London: Harcourt, Brace, Jovanovich, 1977), p. 200.
10. Wald, "Making Sense," p. 386.

Chapter 4

1. Peter Sgroi, *Blue Jeans and Black Robes* (New York: Julian Messner, 1979), pp. 106–17.
2. Ibid., p. 106.
3. Peter C. and Lucille Dunn Kratcoski, "New Perspectives on Juvenile Justice," *Intellect* (June, 1978), pp. 470–72.
4. Robert E. Lee and Carol Klopfer, "Counselors and Juvenile Delinquents: Toward a Comprehensive Treatment Approach," *Personnel and Guidance Journal* (December, 1978), pp. 194–97.
5. Kenneth Keniston, *All Our Children: The American Family Under Pressure* (New York and London: Harcourt, Brace, Jovanovich, 1977), p. 195.
6. Kratcoski and Kratcoski, "New Perspectives," p. 471.
7. Ibid.
8. Lee and Klopfer, "Counselors and Juvenile Delinquents," p. 195.
9. Sgroi, *Blue Jeans,* pp. 62–72.
10. Ibid., pp. 100, 101.
11. Kenneth T. Henson, "Emerging Student Rights," *Journal of Teacher Education,* vol. 30, no. 4 (July-August, 1979), pp. 33–34.
12. Sgroi, *Blue Jeans,* pp. 103–105.

Chapter 5

1. "Teachers on the Picket Line," *Newsweek,* Sept. 10, 1979, p. 70.

NOTES

2. "Cold Shutdown: Chicago's Teacher Walk-out," *Time,* Feb. 11, 1980, p. 53.
3. Chicago *Sun-Times,* Jan. 13, 1980.
4. Martha M. McCarthy, "Court Cases with an Impact on the Teaching of Reading," *Journal of Reading,* vol. 23, no. 3 (December, 1979).
5. Conrad Toepfer, speech given at National College of Education, Ferguson Lectures in Education, March 3, 1980.
   Also Conrad Toepfer, "Brain Growth Periodization—A New Dogma, for Education," *Middle School Journal* (August, 1979), p. 3, 18–20.
6. "Someone Cares About Your Child," South Metropolitan Association, Chicago.
7. "Parent Efforts to Aid the Gifted," New York *Times,* Nov. 11, 1979.
8. Fred M. Hechinger, "About Education: Gifted Children Speak Out," New York *Times,* April 29, 1980.
9. "School Integration: A Long Way to Go," *U. S. News and World Report,* Feb. 26, 1979, p. 13.
10. "24 Years of Integration: Has Busing Really Worked?" *U. S. News and World Report,* May 8, 1978, pp. 43–45.
11. David Armor, "Has Busing Worked?" *Instructor* (March, 1979), p. 24.
12. *Your Legal Rights and Responsibilities* (Village of Winnetka, Ill., 1979).
13. Casey Banas, "Cash—and sympathy—running out for schools," Chicago *Tribune,* April 2, 1980.
14. "Private School Students are Mostly Northern, White, and Wealthy: HEW," *Phi Delta Kappan* (April, 1980), p. 515.
15. Roger Sipher, "Compulsory Education: An Idea Whose Time Has Passed," *USA Today* (September, 1978), pp. 17–19.
16. Richard Ihle, "An Argument for Compulsory Schooling," *Today's Education* (April/May, 1978), pp. 46–47.

Chapter 6

1. Alex Osborn, *Applied Imagination,* 3rd ed. (New York: Charles Schribner and Sons, 1963).
2. K. Chukovsky, *From Two to Five* (Berkeley: University of California Press, 1976), p. 3.
3. Courtney Cazden, *Language in Early Childhood Education*

(Washington, D. C.: National Association for the Education of Young Children, 1972).

4. Clare Cherry, *Creative Play for the Developing Child: Early Lifehood Education Through Play* (Belmont, Calif.: Fearon-Pitman, 1976).

Chapter 7

1. Robert J. Ferullo, "Children's Hypervideo Neuroses," *USA Today,* vol. 107, no. 2408 (May, 1979), p. 57.
2. Nat Rutstein, *Go Watch TV!* (New York: Sheed and Ward, 1974), pp. 173–79.
3. Ferullo, "Neuroses," p. 57.
4. Mac H. Brown, Patsy Skeen, and D. Keith Osborn, "Young Children's Perception of the Reality of Television," *Contemporary Education,* vol. 50, no. 3 (Spring, 1979), p. 129.
5. Jackie S. Busch, "Television's Effects on Reading: A Case Study," *Phi Delta Kappan,* vol. 59, no. 10 (June, 1978), p. 668.
   Also Aletha Huston-Stein and John C. Wright, "Children and Television: Effects of the Medium, Its Content, and Its Form," *Journal of Research and Development in Education,* vol. 13, no. 1 (Spring, 1979), p. 21.
6. Busch, "A Case Study," pp. 668–71.
7. "Kids aren't slaves to television, study says," Chicago *Sun-Times,* March 9, 1980.
8. Nancy Larrick, "TV and Kids: What Teachers are Complaining About," *Learning* (October, 1979), pp. 44–46.
9. Kenneth Keniston, *All Our Children: The American Family Under Pressure* (New York and London: Harcourt, Brace, Jovanovich, 1977), p. 54.
10. Marie Winn, *The Plug-In Drug* (New York: Viking Press, 1977).
11. Larrick, "TV and Kids," p. 45.
12. Dorothy G. Singer, "Reading, Imagination, and Television," *School Library Journal,* vol. 26. no. 4 (December, 1979), pp. 31–34.
13. Ibid., p. 32.
14. Winn, *Plug-In Drug,* p. 51.
15. Ibid., p. 58.
16. Ibid.

NOTES

17. Keniston, *All Our Children* p. 53.
18. Ibid., p. 51.
19. Ibid., p. 53.
20. Charles A. Winick, Lorne G. Williamson, Stuart F. Chuz-mir, and Mariann Pizzella Winick, *Children's TV Commercials: A Content Analysis* (New York, Washington, London: Praeger Publishers, 1973) p. 7.
21. Keniston, *All Our Children*, p. 54.
22. Larrick, "TV and Kids," p. 46.
23. Rutstein, *Go Watch TV!* p. 179.
24. Winn, *Plug-In Drug*, p. 53.
25. Larrick, "TV and Kids," p. 46.
26. Ibid.

Chapter 8

1. "Cult Wars on Capitol Hill," *Time,* Feb. 19, 1979, p. 54.
2. Jack N. Sparks, *The Mindbenders: A Look at Current Cults* (Nashville: Thomas Nelson, 1977), p. 13.
3. Patricia Thomas, "Targets of the Cults," *Human Behavior* (March, 1979), p. 58.
4. Margaret Thaler Singer, "Coming Out of the Cults," *Psychology Today* (January, 1979), p. 75.
5. Gary L. Wall, "A catalog of cults: Where they stand on the deity of Christ," *Moody Monthly,* vol. 79, no. 11 (July/ August, 1979), pp. 20–25.
6. "Europe's Rising Cults," *Newsweek,* May 7, 1979, pp. 100–102.
7. Singer, "Coming Out," p. 82.
8. "Targets of the Cults," p. 58.
9. Singer, "Coming Out," p. 72.
10. "Europe's Rising Cults," pp. 100–102.
11. "Why Do Kids Join the Cults?" *Truth and Countertruth* (Elgin, Ill.: David C. Cook, 1978).
12. "Why youth are heeding the call of the cults," Chicago *Sun-Times,* March 1, 1980.
13. Edward Watkin, "What Makes Children Grow Up Good?" An interview with Dr. Robert Coles, *U.S. Catholic,* vol. 44, no. 8 (August, 1979), pp. 20, 23.
14. Ibid.
15. "Europe's Rising Cults."
16. "Why youth are heeding," *Sun-Times.*

17. Singer "Coming Out," pp. 76, 79.
18. "Cult wars on Capitol Hill."
19. Walter H. Waggoner, "Bar Panel Ponders Dispute Over Cults," New York *Times,* Jan. 25, 1979.
20. Stephen Chapman, "Cult-mongering," *The New Republic,* vol. 180, no. 9 (Feb. 17, 1979), p. 13.

Chapter 9

1. R. Dreikurs, *Children: The Challenge* (New York: Hawthorn Books, 1964).
2. Robert L. DeBruyn, "The Master Teacher," Readership Lane, Manhattan, Kansas 66502.
3. T. Gordon, *Parent Effectiveness Training* (New York: Peter H. Wyden, 1971).
4. H. Ginott, *Between Parent and Child* (New York: Avon, 1965), p. 47.
5. D. Miller, "The Child From Eleven to Fourteen," speech given at the Ferguson Lecture Series, National College of Education, Feb. 4, 1980.

Chapter 10

1. Richard Phillips, "The Sex Game: Kids Play With Life and Pay," Chicago *Tribune,* Nov. 11, 1979.
2. Sol Gordon, ". . . But Where is Sex Education?" *Education Digest* (February, 1978), p. 51.
3. Dr. Hershel D. Thornburg, *The Bubblegum Years: Sticking with Kids from 9–13* (Tucson, Ariz.: H.E.L.P. Books, 1979), p. 114.
4. "Christopher Cory, "Parents' Sexual Silence," *Psychology Today,* vol. 12, no. 8 (January, 1979), p. 14.
5. Roland Summit, and Jo Ann Kryso, "Sexual Abuse of Children: A Clinical Spectrum," *American Journal of Orthopsychiatry,* vol. 48, no. 2 (April, 1978), p. 242.
6. Phillips, "The Sex Game."
7. Ibid.
8. Aaron Hass, "Teens' Teacher? 'Porno,' " Chicago *Sun-Times,* Jan. 16, 1980.
9. Gordon, "Sex Education," p. 51
10. William Mead, and Michael Feinsilber, "The American Way of Sex," *Penthouse* (April, 1980), pp. 163–66.
11. "Sex Education," *Parade,* Feb. 10, 1980.

NOTES

Chapter 12

1. Thomas J. Cottle, "Adolescent Voices: Trying on Adult Masks," *Psychology Today* (February, 1979), p. 40.
2. Alvin Toffler, "A New Kind of Man in the Making," New York *Times Magazine,* March 9, 1980, pp. 24–30.
3. Patricia O'Brien, "With More Parents Working, Who Will Care for the Kids?" Knight-Ridder News Service, 1980.
4. Julius Segal, and Herbert Yahraes, "Protecting Children's Mental Health," *Children Today* (September/October, 1978), pp. 23–25.
5. Kenneth Keniston, *All Our Children: The American Family Under Pressure* (New York and London: Harcourt, Brace, Jovanovich, 1977), p. 23.
6. Segal and Yahraes, "Children's Mental Health," pp. 23–25.

BIBLIOGRAPHY

Adams, Paul; Berg, Leila; Berger, Nan; Duane, Michael; Neill, A.S.; and Ollendorff, Robert. *Children's Rights.* New York and Washington: Praeger, 1971.

Annual Report of the Children's Defense Fund, 1520 New Hampshire Ave., N.W., Washington, D. C. 20036, 1978.

Armor, David. "Has Busing Worked?" *Instructor,* March, 1979.

Boulding, Elise. "Children's Rights." *Society* 15 (November/December, 1977).

Brenton, Myron. "A Further Look at Corporal Punishment." *Today's Education* 67 (November /December, 1978).

Brittain, M. "Inflectional Performance and Early Reading Achievement." *Reading Research Quarterly* 6 (1970).

Brown, Robert Edward. "Therapy on the Air." *Human Behavior* 7 (May, 1978).

Bruner, J. "Poverty and Childhood," in *Preschool in Action: Exploring Early Childhood Programs.* Edited by R. K. Parker. Boston: Allyn & Bacon, 1972.

Calkins, Carl F.; Lukenbill, Ronald W.; and Mateer, William. "Children's Rights: An Introductory Sociological Overview." *Peabody Journal of Education* 50 (January, 1973).

Cazden, Courtney. *Language in Early Childhood Education.* Washington, D. C.: National Association for the Education of Young Children, 1972.

BIBLIOGRAPHY

_____. *Child Language and Education.* Chicago: Holt, Rinehart, and Winston, 1972.

Chapman, Stephen. "Cult-Mongering." *The New Republic* 180 (Feb. 17, 1979).

"Child Abuse and Neglect in the American Society." *The Center Magazine* 2 (April/May, 1978).

Children: in Pursuit of Justice. New York: The Rockefeller Foundation, 1977.

"Children of the World: Rights and Realities." *Social Education* 43 (January, 1979).

Chomsky, C. *The Acquisition of Syntax in Children from 5 to 10.* Cambridge: The MIT Press, 1970.

_____. "Stages in Language Development and Reading Exposure." *Harvard Educational Review* 42 (1972).

Chukovsky, C. *From Two to Five.* Berkeley: University of California Press, 1976.

Collier, Gerald; Tomlinson, Peter; and Wilson, John. *Values and Moral Development in Higher Education.* New York and Toronto: John Wiley & Sons, 1974.

Cory, Christopher. "Parents' Sexual Silence." *Psychology Today,* January, 1979.

Cottle, Thomas J. "Adolescent Voices: "Trying on Adult Masks!" *Psychology Today,* February, 1979.

"Cult Wars on Capitol Hill." *Time,* Feb. 19, 1979.

Danelius, Hans. *Human Rights in Sweden.* Swedish Institute, 1973.

Delattre, Edwin J., and Bennett, William J. "Where the Values Movement Goes Wrong." *CHANGE* 11 (February, 1979).

deLone, Richard H. *Small Futures.* New York and London: Harcourt, Brace, Jovanovich, 1979.

deMause, Lloyd. *The History of Childhood.* New York: Psychohistory Press, 1974.

deSchweinitz, Karl. *Growing Up.* Riverside, N. J.: MacMillan, 1965.

Dobson, James A. *The Strong-Willed Child.* Wheaton, Ill.: Tyndale House, 1978.

Dragonwagon, Crescent. *Wind Rose.* New York: Harper & Row, 1976.

"Europe's Rising Cults." *Newsweek,* May 7, 1979.

Farson, Richard. *Birthrights.* New York: Macmillan, 1974.

189

WHO CONTROLS YOUR CHILD?

Felix, Joseph L. *Parenting with Style.* Huntington, Ind.: Our Sunday Visitor, 1979.

Ferro, Frank. "Addressing Children's Needs." *Children Today* 2 (November/December, 1973).

Feshbach, Norma Deitch and Feshbach, Seymour. "The Changing Status of Children: Rights, Roles & Responsibilities." *Journal of Social Issues* 34 (Spring, 1978).

Frank, Josette. *Television: How to Use It Wisely With Children.* Child Study Association of America, Inc. (1965-1969).

Gallup, George. "The Eleventh Annual Gallup Poll of the Public's Attitudes Toward the Public Schools." *Phi Delta Kappan* 61 (September, 1979).

Giving Youth a Better Chance: Options for Education, Work and Service. Carnegie Council on Policy Studies in Higher Education. San Francisco, Washington, London: Jossey-Bass, 1979.

Goldstein, J.; Freud, A.; and Solnit, A. *Beyond the Best Interests of the Child.* New York: Free Press, 1973.

Gordon, Sol. ". . . But Where is Sex Education?" *Education Digest* (February, 1978).

_____. *Girls are Girls and Boys are Boys: So What's the Difference?* New York: John Day, 1974.

Gragey, William J. *The Psychology of Discipline in the Classroom.* New York: Macmillan, 1968.

Gran, John M. *How to Understand and Teach Teenagers.* Minneapolis: T. S. Denison & Co., 1958.

Gross, Beatrice and Ronald. *The Children's Rights Movement.* Garden City, N.Y.: Anchor Books, 1977.

Hall, Robert T. "Moral Education Today: Progress, Prospects and Problems of a Field Come of Age." *Humanist* 38 (November/December, 1978).

Hass, Aaron. "Love is the Key to Sexual Activity by Teens." Chicago *Sun-Times,* Jan. 16, 1980.

_____. "Teens' Teacher? 'Porno.'" Chicago *Sun-Times,* Jan. 16, 1980.

Henson, Kenneth T. "Emerging Student Rights." *Journal of Teacher Education* 30 (July/August, 1979).

Himmelweit, Hilde T.; Oppenheim, A. N.; and Vince, Pamela. *Television and the Child.* London, New York, Toronto: Oxford University Press, 1958.

Holt, John. *Escape from Childhood: The Needs and Rights of Children.* New York: E. P. Dutton, 1974.

BIBLIOGRAPHY

Ihle, Richard. "An Argument for Compulsory Schooling." *Today's Education* (April/May, 1978).

Jacobson, Ulla. "The Child-Parent Relationship." *Current Sweden,* Swedish Institute (June, 1979).

Jessup, Michael H., and Kiley, Margaret A. *Discipline: Positive Attitudes for Learning.* Englewood Cliffs, N.J.: Prentice Hall, Inc., 1971.

Kelly, Edward J. *Common Sense in Child Raising: A Special Education Approach.* Denver: Lone Publishing Co., 1971.

Keniston, Kenneth. *All Our Children: The American Family Under Pressure.* New York and London: Harcourt, Brace, Jovanovich, 1977.

Klapper, Joseph T. *The Effects of Mass Communication.* New York: The Free Press, 1963.

Kratcoski, Peter C, and Dunn, Lucille. "New Perspectives on Juvenile Justice." *Intellect* (June, 1978).

Kroth, Roger L. *Communicating with Parents of Exceptional Children.* Denver: Lone Publishing Co., 1975.

Lee, Robert E., and Klopfer, Carol. "Counselors and Juvenile Delinquents: Toward a Comprehensive Treatment Approach." *Personnel & Guidance Journal* (December, 1978).

Lerrigo, Mario O., and Southard, Helen. "Parents Responsibility." Prepared for the Joint Committee on Health Problems in Education of the National Education Association and the American Medical Association (1970).

Lewis, Ken. "On Reducing the Snatching Syndrome." *Children Today* 7 (November/December, 1978).

Loban, W. D. *The Language of Elementary School Children.* Champaign, Ill.: National Council of Teachers of English, Research Report No. 1, 1963.

Mander, Jerry. *Four Arguments for the Elimination of Television.* New York: Morrow Quill Paperbacks, 1978.

Marker, Gail, and Friedman, Paul R. "Rethinking Children's Rights." *Children Today* 2 (November/December, 1973).

Marker, Gerald W., and Risinger, C. Frederick. "Top Priority in the Family Agenda: A Global Perspective." *Children Today* 7 (September/October, 1978).

Mayhew, Lewis B. *Surviving the Eighties.* San Francisco, Washington, London: Jossey-Bass, 1979.

Mayle, Peter. *Where Did I Come From?* Secaucus, N. J.: Lyle Stuart, 1973.

Mead, William, and Feinsilber, Michael. "The American Way of Sex," *Penthouse*, April, 1980.

Melody, William. *Children's Television*. New Haven and London: Yale University Press, 1973.

Muson, Howard. "Blind Obedience." *Psychology Today*, January, 1978.

―――――. "Moral Thinking: Can It Be Taught?" *Psychology Today*, February, 1979.

Niensted, Serena. "Discipline for Today's Different Children." *Phi Delta Kappan* 60 (April, 1979).

Nilsson, Lennart. *How Was I Born?* New York: Delacorte Press, 1975.

Orden, Phyllis Van. "Question of Children's Rights: A Bibliography." *School Media Quarterly* 7 (Winter, 1979).

Osborn, Alex, *Applied Imagination,* 3rd ed. New York: Charles Scribner and Sons, 1963.

Phillips, Richard. "The Sex Game: Kids Play with Life and Pay." Chicago *Tribune,* Nov. 11, 1979.

Piaget, J. *The Origins of Intelligence in the Child.* London: Routledge & Kegan Paul, 1953.

Pines, Maya. "Invisible Playmates." *Psychology Today,* September, 1978.

Postman, Neil, and Weingartner, Charles. *Teaching As a Subversive Activity.* New York: Delacorte Press, 1969.

"Rights of Children: Human and Legal." *Peabody Journal of Education* 50 (January, 1973).

"Rights of Foster Children." *Children Today* 2 (July/August, 1973).

Rokeach, Milton. *Beliefs, Attitudes and Values.* San Francisco, Washington, London: Jossey-Bass, 1976.

Rosenfield, Albert. "The 'Elastic Mind' Movement: Rationalizing Child Neglect?" *Saturday Review,* April 1, 1978.

Rutstein, Nat. *Go Watch TV!* New York: Sheed and Ward, 1974.

Salzer, E. Michael. "The Child's Right to Play." *Current Sweden,* Swedish Institute (May, 1979).

―――――. "To Combat Violence in the Child's World." *Current Sweden,* Swedish Institute (July, 1979).

Schimmel, David, and Fischer, Louis. "Discipline and Due Process in the Schools." *Educational Digest* 43 (January, 1978).

"The Search for Fulfillment." *Intellect* (May, 1978).

Segal, Julius, and Yahraes, Herbert. "Protecting Children's Mental Health." *Children Today* 7 (September/October, 1978).

BIBLIOGRAPHY

Sgroi, Peter. *Blue Jeans and Black Robes.* New York: Julian Messner, 1979.

Shane, Harold G. "Education in Transformation: Major Developments of the 'Uneasy Eighties' (in Retrospect)." *Phi Delta Kappan* (December, 1979).

Sheviakov, George V., and Redl, Fritz. *Discipline: For Today's Children & Youth.* Washington, D.C.: Association for Supervision & Curriculum Development, 1944, 1956.

Simon, Sidney B.; Howe, Leland W.; and Kirschenbaum, Howard. *Values Clarification.* New York: Hart, 1972.

Singer, Margaret Thaler. "Coming Out of the Cults." *Psychology Today,* January, 1979.

Snyder, Phyllis R., and Martin, Lawrence H. "Leaving the Family Out of Family Court: Criminalizing the Juvenile Justice System" *American Journal of Orthopsychiatry* (July, 1978).

Soman, Shirley. *Let's Stop Destroying Our Children.* New York: Hawthorn Books, 1974.

"Someone Cares About Your Child." South Metropolitan Association, Chicago.

Sparks, Jack N. *The Mindbenders: A Look at Current Cults.* Nashville: Thomas Nelson, 1977.

Spiel, Oskar. *Discipline Without Punishment.* London: Faber & Faber, 1962.

Stachowiak, Robert J. "Children's Rights: Social Reality or Utopian Ideal?" *Peabody Journal of Education* 50 (June, 1973).

Stein, Sara B. *Making Babies.* New York: Walker and Co., 1970.

Strickland, R. "The Language of Elementary Children. Its Relationship to the Language of Reading Textbooks and the Quality of Reading of Selected Children." *Bulletin of the School of Education,* Indiana University, 1962.

Sullivan, Eileen S. "After Tinker: The Student's Right to Free Expression." *Wilson Library Bulletin* 51 (October, 1976).

Summit, Roland, and Kryso, Jo Ann. "Sexual Abuse of Children: A Clinical Spectrum," *American Journal of Orthopsychiatry* 48 (April, 1978).

Sutton, Thomas L. "Human Rights and Children." *Educational Theory* 28 (Spring, 1978).

Thomas, Patricia. "Targets of the Cults." *Human Behavior,* March, 1979.

Thornburg, Dr. Hershel D. *The Bubblegum Years: Sticking with Kids from 9–13.* Tucson, Arizona: H.E.L.P. Books, 1979.

Toepfer, Conrad. "Brain Growth Periodization—A New Dogma for Education." *Middle School Journal* (August, 1979).

WHO CONTROLS YOUR CHILD?

Toffler, Alvin. "A New Kind of Man in the Making." *New York Times Magazine,* March 9, 1980.

Vardin, Patricia A., and Brody, Ilene N. *Children's Rights: Contemporary Perspectives.* New York and London: Teachers College Press, 1979.

Vigore, Vanessa. "Signals of Child Abuse." *Day Care and Early Education* 5 (Spring, 1978).

Vygotsky, L. *Thought and Language.* Edited and translated by E. Haufman and G. Vakar. Cambridge: The MIT Press, 1962.

Waggoner, Walter H. "Bar Panel Ponders Dispute Over Cults." New York *Times,* Jan. 25, 1979.

Wald, Pat. "Making Sense Out of the Rights of Youth." *Child Welfare* 55 (June, 1976).

Wall, Gary L. "A Catalog of Cults: Where They Stand on the Diety of Christ." *Moody Monthly,* July/August, 1979.

Walzer, Michael. "Teaching Morality. *The New Republic,* June 10, 1978.

Wasserman, Laurie Joseph. "Schooling and the Rights of Children." *School Review* 85 (August, 1977).

Watkin, Edward. "What Makes Children Grow Up Good?" An interview with Dr. Robert Coles. *U.S. Catholic,* August, 1979.

Weinberg, Dr. S. Kirson. *Incest Behavior.* New Jersey: Citadel Press, 1955.

Wiggin, Kate Douglas. *Children's Rights.* Boston and New York: Houghton, Mifflin & Co., 1892.

Wilkerson, Albert E. *The Rights of Children: Emergent Concepts in Law & Society.* Philadelphia: Temple University Press, 1973.

Williams, Avon N. Jr. "Does a Child Have a Right Not to be Brainwashed by Adults?" *Peabody Journal of Education* 50 (January, 1973).

Williams, John W. "Discipline in the Public Schools." *Phi Delta Kappan* 60 (January, 1979).

Williams, Maureen Smith. "The Year of the Child: Did It Do Any Good?" *McCalls,* December, 1979.

Winn, Marie. *The Plug-In Drug.* New York: Viking Press, 1977.

"Why Do Kids Join the Cults?" *Truth & Countertruth,* Elgin, Ill.: David C. Cook, 1978.

"Why Youth are Heeding the Call of the Cults," Chicago *Sun-Times,* March 1, 1980.

Wolff, Anthony. "How to Teach Your Child to Trust." *Parents' Magazine,* November, 1978.